INVITATION TO JOHN

A Short-Term **DISCIPLE** Bible Study

INVITATION TO JOHN

PARTICIPANT BOOK

Robert D. Kysar

Abingdon Press
Nashville

A number of its features makes a study of John difficult. Among the most important is that John seems to use the word *disciple* to refer to any believer, implying that discipleship is the essence of Christian life, not a special calling. Discipleship is clearly divinely empowered in the Gospel of John. God chooses the believers and "gives" them to Christ. The Holy Spirit is described in new language as "the Counselor" or "the Advocate." The Jesus depicted in John speaks in different ways, often in figures of speech and in long passages. Running throughout the Gospel is a theme scholars call the "misunderstanding motif." Again and again Jesus speaks in such a way as to confuse characters in the story (and often readers as well). One has to probe a bit to clarify Jesus' meaning. An example is the way Jesus uses the expression *born from above* in the discussion with Nicodemus in John 3.

In the Synoptic Gospels, Jesus most often speaks in relatively short sayings, and the longer speeches look as if they are a collection of many of the shorter sayings (for instance, the Sermon on the Mount in Matthew 5:1–7:29). In John, however, Jesus' speeches are often long and confusing. He seems to speak in what we might call a "stream of consciousness" style in which the connections between individual parts are not necessarily logical at all.

John is often the Gospel given to Christians new to the faith; but in fact it is not the simplest of the four to understand. Yet it is so important and unique that I invite you to come with us on a journey through the Gospel. Come and see the Jesus who calls and talks, argues and prays, breaks bread and washes feet. Come and see what it means to follow the Jesus who claims to be living water, the true light, the way, the truth, and the life—our life.

Come and See

When Jesus turned and saw them following, he said to them,
"What are you looking for?" They said to him, "Rabbi"
(which translated means Teacher), "where are you staying?"
He said to them, "Come and see."

—John 1:38-39

INTRODUCTION

Think of a time when friends told you about a beautiful place or sight, but you were hesitant to believe that it was as gorgeous as they described it. You were hesitant to believe them because you wanted to experience it for yourself. When John the Baptizer declares, "Look, here is the Lamb of God!" (1:36), two of those who will become disciples are at first only curious. "Where are you staying?" they ask Jesus. Jesus responds simply by saying, "Come and see" (1:38-39). The two soon-to-be disciples do what Jesus says, and a chain reaction begins. By the end of Chapter 1, there are five men—at first only curious—who follow Jesus. Yet before they moved in Jesus' direction, they had to see for themselves!

COME AND SEE

In the first chapter of the Gospel of John, Jesus' simple invitation to "come and see" is intriguing. First, it introduces the theme of seeing, which appears throughout the narrative. Second, it seems this invitation language is prompted by the question of where Jesus is staying. It seems a simple question, but it hints at something more. The word *staying* translates the Greek word *menein* (MA-NAYN), which takes on several meanings in John's Gospel. The word is often translated "abide," as in Jesus' metaphor about the vine and branches in 15:1-7. An interesting side note here is that in John 14:2, the term *dwelling places* (those in God's house) is a translation of the Greek noun *monai* (MO-NAY), which is based on the verb form used in John 1 to mean "stay" or "remain."

A TIME BEFORE TIME

Before we get too far ahead of ourselves in these first two chapters, we should linger a moment on that fascinating passage in 1:1-18, known as the Prologue. John begins his Gospel with the summons to imagine a mysterious "beginning"—the time before time. The passage reads like poetry, evoking emotions of all kinds. John's words are chosen to leave hearers awestruck, contemplating the picture of the "Word" (*logos*, LA-GAHS) alongside that of God. Through the activity of this *logos*, this Word, who is both "life" and "light," God creates all that is. John declares that "the Word *was with* God, and the Word *was* God" (1:1, italics added for emphasis). What can this mean? Could it be that the most important meaning of *logos* is that this Word (Jesus) brought into the world the possibility of living as God always intended for us to live?

Reading further in the Prologue, notice the opposition of light and darkness in 1:4-5. It is the first of a whole group of what we might call opposing realities. John 1:6-8 makes clear that John the Baptizer is not the light but rather the witness to the light. It is quite likely that some thought John the Baptizer himself was the long-awaited Messiah.

The light of the *logos* intrudes into the world but is rejected by "his own" (1:11). Yet, those who accept him are given a unique power—a power (or authority) to become who they are really meant to be. Rejected though he is, the *logos* becomes a flesh-and-blood human being who "camped out" (a more literal translation of the word translated as "lived" in the NRSV) with us in this world. Through him, believers are able to see God's "glory."

In other words, for those who believe in him, the incarnate Word shows them who God is.

Another reference to John the Baptizer's witness (1:15) is followed by the climax of the Prologue's introduction. Christ brought "grace and truth" (1:17) into the world. The *logos* brought us a means of connecting or identifying with God's loving intention for humanity. (It might be compared with how three-dimensional glasses enable us to see depth as well as height and length.) The gift of grace and truth supplements the will of God for human behavior revealed by Moses. However, let there be no doubt: Christ alone has seen God (Exodus 33:18–23), for he originates in the very heart of God.

This dramatic and provocative introduction sets a tone for the whole Gospel. It invites us to look for God's purpose for us and our world as we read this account of Jesus, God's Word to the world.

THE BAPTIZER'S MESSAGE

The Prologue of the Gospel introduces us to John the Baptizer (1:6-8, 15). Now we get some more details. The religious authorities send representatives to find out just who Jesus thinks he is. Notice that in 1:19 these representatives are said to be sent by the Jews. In 1:24, however, the examiners are sent out by the Pharisees. This is one of the clearest examples of how John uses "the Jews" to speak of religious authorities. We will return to this question later.

John the Baptizer makes plain that he does not pretend to be Christ (that is, the Messiah). After rejecting the notion that he is Elijah, in 1:23 John simply says he is "the voice of one crying out in

Pharisees

The Gospels are critical of the Pharisees, but in fact they were a devout group of Jewish laymen who sought to obey the Law fully. They voluntarily took on themselves the obligation to obey the laws applicable only to the priests. They were not self-righteous but were trying to determine what it meant to be faithful to God. They were the church's first opponents, but they should not be taken as typical of the Jewish people.

Hour

Refers to the time of Jesus' arrest, trial, crucifixion, and resurrection. The statement *His hour had not yet come* is scattered throughout the chapters of John, along with the promise that the hour will eventually come and finally the announcement that it has come.

- The hour has not come – 2:4; 7:30; 8:20.

- The hour is promised – 4:21, 23; 5:25, 28; 16:2, 25.

- The hour comes – 12:23; 13:1; 16:32.

addressing a woman. His point is to make clear that neither he nor his mother should assume responsibility for the shortage of wine at the wedding, implying even that it would be presumptuous to do so.

Second, Jesus seems hesitant to do anything because his "hour has not yet come" (John 2:4). At this early stage in the narrative, we have no clue as to what that statement means. However, we will soon learn that when Jesus speaks the word *hour*, he means the decisive time, the climactic moment, and the occasion of his death.

Third, the incident is called a sign, or in John's Greek *sēmeia* (SAY-MAY-AH), a term intended to evoke the disciples' faith (2:11). Again, we will need to watch for future occurrences of this word. For now, it is enough to recognize that by "sign" Jesus and John mean an act by which Jesus' identity is revealed. In turning water into wine, Jesus powerfully demonstrates the glory of his relationship with God.

CLEANING OUT THE TEMPLE

At last we come to a story common to all the Gospels (Matthew 21:12-17; Mark 11:15-18; Luke 19:45-46; John 2:13-23). But what is it doing so early in John's narrative? For the Synoptic Gospel writers, Jesus' cleansing of the Temple was an event associated with the final days of his ministry, and it took place during his first and only trip to Jerusalem. Regardless of the timing, though, all four Gospels connect the event with the Jewish Passover, one of the high holy days for Jewish worshipers, just as it continues to be to this day. Passover recalls and reenacts that final dreadful plague visited on the Egyptians as a means of freeing the Hebrew people from their slavery. The angel of death moved among the Egyptians, killing every firstborn child but "passing over" the Jews' homes, where the doors were marked with the blood of a lamb. Passover is the occasion on which all the Gospels say Jesus was arrested, tried, and crucified. However, in John's story of Jesus, the incident in the Temple occurs during the first of Jesus' three visits to Jerusalem for the celebration of the Passover.

As all four Gospels report, Jesus drove the money changers out of the Temple grounds. These "business men" exchanged foreign coins for the Jewish money used in the Temple and sold pigeons (or, as John has it, sheep and cattle) for ritual sacrifices. These clever men made the most of the predicament of the Jews who came to Jerusalem from all around the Mediterranean world for this occasion. (We need not travel far before we learn to beware those who claim to offer a generous exchange rate for our money.) John reports that Jesus fashioned a whip with which he could drive the animals off the Temple grounds. Much like the story in the Synoptic Gospels, Jesus declares that this sacred place—"my Father's house" (2:16)—should not be a trading place. The occasion reminds the disciples of Psalm 69:9.

> ### Sign
>
> **A deed by means of which Jesus shows his true identity. Often the deed is a wondrous act, such as a healing. However, Jesus is cautious about the response of people to his signs, suggesting that a faith based on signs is not genuine (see 4:48). Eight acts are considered signs in John: 2:1-11; 4:46-54; 5:1-9; 6:1-14; 6:15-21; 9:1-8; 11:1-46; and 21:1-14.**

The Gospels of Mark and Luke say that the response to Jesus' presumptuous act was the effort to have him killed. In John, it sparks a lively discussion between him and the Jews. What right does he have to upset a regular Passover custom? What are his credentials? Jesus counters with an enigmatic and puzzling statement: "Destroy this temple, and in three days I will raise it up" (John 2:19). Here is our first clear occurrence of a favorite theme in John: Jesus makes a statement of some sort (often figurative), and the hearers misunderstand it. In this case, the religious authorities naturally think he is referring to the Temple structure that was not even finished at the time. The effort to rebuild Solomon's Temple began soon after its destruction by the Babylonians around 587–586 B.C. During Jesus' life, it was now undergoing renovations

FOR FURTHER REFLECTION

One of the roots of the concept of the Word (logos) in John 1:1-18 is the Jewish notion of Wisdom (*sophia*, SO-FE-AH). The apocryphal books of the Old Testament are a collection of documents, many of which were included in some editions of the Bible. One of these books is Ecclesiasticus, or the Wisdom of Jesus, Son of Sirach, which dates from around 180 B.C. Portions of the book have to do with an understanding of Wisdom in Jewish thought just before the birth of Christianity. The following quotation from Sirach shows the connections between the ideas of *sophia* (Wisdom) and *logos* (Word). The passage supposes that Wisdom existed before creation and talks about how Wisdom is dwelling in the earth, sounding much like John's use of the Greek word *skānoō* (SKAY-NAH-AH-O), meaning "tenting" in John 1:14 to describe Jesus' incarnation.

> Wisdom praises herself, / and tells of her glory in the midst of the people. / In the assembly of the Most High she opens her mouth, / and in the presence of his hosts she tells of her glory:…"Then the Creator of all things gave me a command, / and my Creator chose the place for my tent. / He said, 'Make your dwelling in Jacob, / and in Israel receive your inheritance.' / Before the ages, in the beginning, he created me, / and for all the ages I shall not cease to be. / In the holy tent I ministered before him, / and so I was established in Zion.   —Sirach 24:1-2, 8-10

How do the ideas of Wisdom and Word connect? What do they have in common? Reflect on how living in and for Christ entails a special kind of Wisdom.

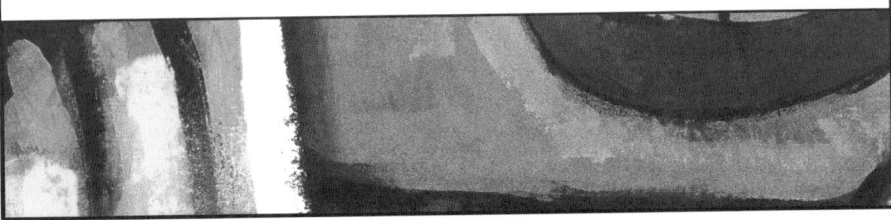

How Is It Possible?

Jesus answered, "Very truly, I tell you, no one can enter the kingdom of God without being born of water and Spirit." ...Nicodemus said to him, "How can these things be?"

—John 3:5, 9

INTRODUCTION

Contemporary life is filled with so many wondrous possibilities: genetics, space travel, modern medicine, the Internet—even the ubiquitous cell phone. I write these words in one part of the country and will send them instantly to an editor hundreds of miles away! The list goes on and on. More and more the seemingly impossible becomes possible.

However, that doesn't mean we are not still confronted with experiences or claims that make us ask, "How is it possible?" Our Christian faith sometimes leads us to ask that very question. Is it possible that God really hears the prayers of all the people in the world—even the prayers of those of other religions? Is it possible that the church is still influential in this time and place? Is it possible to believe that our witness to the good news of Jesus Christ amounts to anything? The story of Nicodemus's midnight conversation with Jesus invites us to ask what we think is possible and what we think is impossible.

DAILY ASSIGNMENTS

DAY ONE: John 3:1-15

Why does Nicodemus fail to understand what Jesus says? Why does he respond by asking, "How can anyone be born after having grown old?" (3:4), and "How can these things be?" (3:9)? When have you said, "How is it possible?"

DAY TWO: John 3:16-21

Nicodemus leaves the scene, and Jesus launches into an extended speech. What connections do you see between this speech and Jesus' conversation with Nicodemus? How would you explain the view of judgment expressed in 3:18-21?

DAY THREE: John 3:22-36

What do these verses tell us about John the Baptizer? What is the meaning of the metaphor of the bridegroom and the friend of the bridegroom in 3:29-30? Read Isaiah 62:5; Jeremiah 2:2; and Hosea 2:16-20 and note how the bride and bridegroom are used there. How does John 3:36 seem to summarize what has been said in 3:22-35?

DAY FOUR: John 4:1-30

Compare and contrast the conversation Jesus has with the Samaritan woman and the one he has with Nicodemus. What would you say is the point of the story of the Samaritan woman and Jesus? How would you explain the significance of the image of living water? Read Exodus 3:14 and Isaiah 43:10-11; 51:12. How do these passages help define Jesus' use of the "I am" expression? Why is the woman's witness to Jesus that she makes to others in her village effective? What can we learn from her witness that would strengthen our own witness?

DAY FIVE: John 4:31-54

Reflect on Jesus' words about the harvest in 4:35-38. What do the metaphors of the sower and reaper have to do with the setting in which they appear? How would you summarize the point of the metaphors for those who know little about farming? How might the healing of the official's son be viewed as an incident of "reaping"? What are the most interesting and striking features of the story of the healing of the official's son? What does this story tell us about John's representation of what Jesus thought of "signs and wonders" (4:48)?

DAY SIX:

Read the commentary in the participant book.

OUT OF THE DARKNESS

In John 3, Jesus' conversation with Nicodemus is puzzling and has stimulated a great deal of commentary among Bible students and scholars. One of the main questions is whether to understand Nicodemus's arrival at night as a way of saying that he lived in the darkness of unbelief or simply that he secretly sought Jesus out—or both.

Jesus seemingly befuddles Nicodemus with his use of ambiguous words. When Jesus declares, "No one can see the kingdom of God without being born from above" (3:3), he uses the Greek word *anōthen* (AN-O-THIN), which can mean "again," "anew," or "from above." Then he speaks of being born of water and the Spirit but immediately speaks of the wind (3:6-8). The word translated as "Spirit" is *pneuma* (NEW-MAH), which also means wind. (The blowing of the wind becomes a metaphor for the freedom of the Spirit.) In 3:14, Jesus tells Nicodemus that the "Son of Man" will "be lifted up." With deliberate irony, John was probably saying that Jesus' crucifixion was also his enthronement as king.

Lifted Up

The phrase *lifted up* translates the Greek word *hypsaō* (HUPS-AH-O) and was used to describe both the lifting of one up onto a king's throne and the raising of a cross. John uses the word to summarize how Jesus was put to death and how that death meant he was exalted to lordship.

Notice that Nicodemus's contributions to the conversation are limited to "How is it possible?" (3:2, 4, 9.) At one time or another, have we not asked Jesus the same question? After he finally disappears into the darkness again, Nicodemus steps briefly back into view only twice more, in 7:45-52 and 19:38-42. In light of these later appearances, it is not clear whether or not Jesus' nighttime visitor ever became a believer.

Once Nicodemus departs, Jesus begins speaking of God's mission in the world through him and the assurance that God does not seek to condemn the world (3:16-20). We condemn ourselves depending upon how we respond to the light. By refusing the light, we destine ourselves to lives deprived of purpose and strength. In this case, condemnation is not so much a miserable eternity in a hell as it is a pointless life lived without true purpose and direction. Do we hide from God for fear of what we may learn about ourselves should God enlighten us?

JOHN THE BAPTIZER'S FINALE

The next scene (3:22-36) moves us back to John the Baptizer, this time for his last appearance in John's Gospel. The story begins with an acknowledgement that Jesus baptized some followers. Along with 4:1-2, this is the only statement that Jesus baptized anyone. However, 4:2 confuses us by claiming that it was only Jesus' disciples, not Jesus himself, who baptized! There is no easy resolution to this contradiction. Some think the author wrote that Jesus *did* baptize, and a later editor added the denial. John 3:24 acknowledges that John the Baptizer would be imprisoned, even though the Gospel of John never reports his imprisonment (see Matthew 11:2-3; Mark 6:17-18; Luke 3:18-20).

The question of John's and Jesus' baptisms raises the issue of purification (3:25). In spite of some of his followers, John the Baptizer refuses to become Jesus' competitor. His words clearly indicate his subservience to Jesus; he compares himself with the friend of the groom at a wedding as opposed to the groom himself (3:28-29). The whole question is resolved in terms of what God has given each leader. John the Baptizer summarizes the discussion with the declaration that Jesus "must increase" and he "must decrease" (3:30).

> *Eternal Life*
>
> A life that is in accord with the will of God for humans. Refers not so much to the length of life as to its quality.
> See John 3:16.

In 3:31-36, the Gospel provides a nice digest of the author's view of Jesus and his relationship with God. Christ comes from heaven and is sent by God to speak God's words. The relationship is based on God's love of the Son. John uses verse 36 to tie verses 31-35 together: To believe in Christ is to embrace "eternal life," but to deny Christ is to lose the opportunity to live the life the Creator intended.

In the final sections of John 3, the Baptizer is a major witness to God's revelation through the divine Word. The witness is simply this: Belief in the message that God sends through Christ empowers us to live as the Creator intended us to live (see 1:12).

WATER, WATER, EVERYWHERE

The Gospel of John uses some of the basic human physical needs (such as water and food) as symbols of God's gift to us in Christ. In the conversation violating at least two social regulations and crossing at least two lines of social custom. Certainly for John, this Jesus would not be boxed in by practices that separated people from one another.

In the meantime, the woman has left her water jar (no longer important to her) and returned to her village. There she shares her exciting news, but in a delightfully exaggerated way: "Come and see a man who told me everything I have ever done! He cannot be the Messiah, can he?" (4:29). Our experiences with Christ often stir the kind of excitement that ignores the boundaries of exactitude. And look at the results of the woman's excitement: The villagers follow her back to the well to see for themselves. Even though Nicodemus (the religious leader) failed to understand Jesus at all, the Samaritan woman is a bright and verbal discussion partner. Here we see more of John's irony.

Standing on the periphery of the story, the disciples come onto the scene, simply wanting Jesus to have something to eat. But for Jesus, "food" takes on a deeper meaning than physical nourishment alone (4:31-34). Jesus makes clear to his disciples that doing the will of God provides another kind of sustenance—for Jesus as well as for them. The image of food connects Jesus' words in 4:34 with what he says next: "But I tell you, look around you, and see how the fields are ripe for harvesting" (4:35). Here is the common image for those of an agricultural society—sowing seed and harvesting (see, for instance, Luke 8:4-15). Remember that when Jesus calls attention to the fields ready for harvest, he and the disciples are—of all places—in Samaria.

What follows in 4:36-38 is a little lesson in Christian witness. Jesus reminds his followers, then and now, that some may not be the sowers but still have the privilege of sharing in the reaping. We are always dependent on others who have gone before us. The Samaritan woman sows the seeds of faith that reach maturity only when the villagers encounter Jesus for themselves. Jesus remains in the village for two days, and the residents see for themselves what the woman had announced to them. In their witness, the villagers name Jesus in a new but most appropriate way: "Savior of the world" (4:42). In the process of Christian maturation, there comes a time when we must experience for ourselves what we have heard from others.

BELIEVING THE WORD

Back in Galilee, Jesus experiences what it means for a prophet to be honored everywhere but back home (see Mark 6:1-6 for a more detailed account of this). Yet in spite of that, John records that the Galileans believe in him because they had seen what Jesus did in Jerusalem. We are left to resolve the contradiction between 4:44 and 45: Is Jesus both rejected and welcomed in Galilee? The best that can be said is that the belief of the Galileans was based on a superficial response to Jesus' marvelous deeds. And if such is the case, John 4:43-45 is a good introduction to the healing of the official's son that follows.

We are not told precisely what sort of "royal official" (4:46) comes to Jesus (see Matthew 8:5-13 for clues). The point is that he is a prominent figure brought to despair and helplessness by the illness of his dying son. Surprisingly, Jesus rebukes him at first for needing signs on which to base his faith; but the official is not dissuaded. Jesus finally declares that his son is healed and the official should return home. The key statement in this story is "The man believed the word that Jesus spoke to him" (4:50b). Without certainty that his son is healed, the official takes Jesus on his word. His faith is "word faith" as opposed to "signs faith." In this way, the official's response to Jesus' words plays an important role in John's Gospel. When the official learns that his son was indeed healed the very hour Jesus had spoken these words, his faith is affirmed. John tells us this was the second of Jesus' signs in Galilee. And so in this story, we see an example of faith not based on an experience of God's action but based solely on God's word, specifically on God's promise of active love.

INVITATION TO DISCIPLESHIP

What marvelous examples of discipleship we have in John the Baptizer and the Samaritan woman. John the Baptizer sets aside all his own ambitions to witness to Christ. His finger points not to himself but to the Word made flesh. His single-mindedness provides us a model for our own witness. The Samaritan woman is evidence of the long reach of the arms of God's grace and love in Christ, a reach that stretches beyond all the social boundaries we have constructed that so often constrain us. As if to counter a male-dominated church, this woman reveals the all-inclusiveness of God's love and a pattern for our contemporary discipleship. She is neither perfect nor pious; she is simply an inviting witness. Together, both John the Baptizer and the Samaritan woman stand out as living responses to Nicodemus's troubled inquiry, "How is it possible?"

Taste for Yourself

[Jesus said,] "The bread of God is that which comes down from heaven and gives life to the world." They said to him, "Sir, give us this bread always."

—John 6:33-34

INTRODUCTION

Many of us are skeptical of others' claims that a particular food is delicious. Sushi may taste scrumptious to you, but not necessarily to me. There is really no substitute for tasting something for ourselves. While my wife and I were in China, we were somewhat skeptical of the prospects of eating some of the delicacies we were served. Yet, by the time we concluded our visit in China, we had grown especially fond of some of the local cuisine. John 5–6 makes outrageous claims for Jesus and who he is. In a sense, these chapters invite us to "taste" and decide for ourselves who Jesus is and what he is like.

DAILY ASSIGNMENTS

DAY ONE: John 5:1-18

What are the most striking features of this account of Jesus' healing? Why does Jesus ask the lame man if he wants to be healed (5:6), and why does the man not know who healed him (5:13)? Read Exodus 20:8-11; 31:12-17; 35:2-3; and Deuteronomy 5:12-15. Consider how these Old Testament passages help explain the religious leaders' reaction to Jesus' action in this story. Read Jeremiah 31:29-30 and Ezekiel 18:1-4. How do those passages help you interpret John 5:14?

sin → bad things punishment

DAY TWO: John 5:19-30

These verses seem to be a reply to 5:18, where John says the religious leaders sought to kill Jesus. Summarize what you understand to be Jesus' response. Read about Jeremiah's rejection by his people (Jeremiah 18:18-23). How is Jeremiah's experience like that of Jesus? What do you think John 5:24 means? How does that verse fit into your own view of life after death?

Crossed over from death to life — ? body resurrected when Christ returns

DAY THREE: John 5:31-47

In this passage, Jesus seems to be justifying his actions by reference to those who witness (or testify) to him. Read Deuteronomy 19:15 and consider how that passage determines some of what Jesus says here. Why does Jesus appeal to Moses in John 5:45-37? Read Micah 6:1-8, where God is said to put the people of Israel on trial, and they are invited to plead their case. Why are trial and witness so important?

DAY FOUR: John 6:1-21

After reading these verses, read the Synoptic Gospels' accounts of Jesus' feeding a multitude: Matthew 14:13-21 and 15:32-39; Mark 6:30-44 and 8:1-10; Luke 9:10-17. Then go back and read the story in John again. Make note of what stands out as unique in John's version. How does the story of Jesus walking on water influence your interpretation of the feeding story?

-gather leftovers

—

DAY FIVE: John 6:22-71

This passage begins a long dialogue between Jesus and various members of the crowd. Read Exodus 16 to get a perspective on John 6:22-71. Now read through the whole discussion and make a list of the different groups with whom Jesus discusses his role. Summarize what each group says in response to Jesus and his words. What is Jesus' purpose in speaking of eating his flesh and drinking his blood in this passage? Some of Jesus' "disciples" are offended by his words and no longer associate with him. What does this tell us about how John uses the word *disciple*?

disciple— all followers

people
Jews (religious leaders)

DAY SIX:

Read the commentary in the participant book.

A HANDICAPPED WALKER?

Following on the heels of the healing of the royal official's son in John 4 comes the healing of a disabled man in a pool. The site of the event is carefully described and has enabled historians (and archaeologists) to locate the possible setting for the healing in contemporary Jerusalem. On rare occasions, a stream entering the pools caused the waters to bubble up. The ill and disabled bathed in the water in hopes that it would heal them. Even the best medical care can only heal if it is accompanied by a patient's genuine desire to be healed. That fact seems to be part of the reason for Jesus' rather strange question to the man in John 5:6. Like many of the healing stories in the Gospels, the evidence of the man's healing is the fact that he carries his sleeping bag as he walks away.

Jesus' statement to the man during a later encounter complicates matters. In 5:14, Jesus exhorts the man to sin no more "so that nothing worse happens to you." (Compare this with what Jesus says later in 9:3.) The notion that sin causes suffering is deeply rooted in the Old Testament (see Psalm 38:3); and in first-century Jewish thought, human ailments were often believed to be evidence of sin. The Synoptic Gospels also refer to this cause-and-effect relationship between sin and calamity (see Luke 13:1-5). Even today, Christians—non-Christians too—are prone to explain suffering as the result of sin or some kind of moral wrongdoing.

Religious customs and pragmatic realities are not always harmonious. In Jesus' day, healing was regarded as work and was therefore prohibited on the sabbath (unless life depended on immediate care). In the case in John 5, the violation may be in the man's carrying his bed. The religious leaders are often criticized for their concern to obey the sabbath law, but they are representative of the way in which religious custom dictates practice. In that sense, they are perhaps no more legalistic than we sometimes are. Jesus' response to criticism of his healing activity is a simple one: God doesn't take a day off, so neither does he (5:16-17).

Whatever the case, Jesus finds himself in a confrontational discussion of healing on the sabbath. More importantly, though, he offends the religious leaders by "making himself equal to God" (5:18).

WHO DO YOU THINK YOU ARE?

When others speak and/or act like they are absolute authorities on certain issues, we naturally question their understanding of themselves. When the religious leaders accuse Jesus of acting as if he is above the Law, he responds with a statement on the relationship of the Father and the Son. He claims he only mimics what God does. This leads him to speak of the matter of life and death and make some interesting claims. First, those who believe in the Son have "eternal life" and have passed beyond judgment (5:24). So it sounds like eternal life is in the believer's present. But wait! In 5:25-29, Jesus speaks of a future resurrection from the dead and of a judgment that occurs when the "hour" has come. Now it sounds like new life is in the believer's *future*. So which is it—or, is it somehow both? Of course, the point is that Jesus is God's special agent in the world and is himself God.

WITNESSES FOR THE DEFENSE

We cannot testify for ourselves and expect others to believe us. In Jewish practice, self-witness was not allowed, and one witness was not enough to condemn someone of a crime (Deuteronomy 19:15). Having made such high claims for himself in the previous verses, Jesus now calls to the stand five witnesses on his behalf (John 5:33-47):

- John the Baptizer (5:33-35)

- Jesus' own works that defend his claims (5:36)

- God (5:37-38)

- Scripture, meaning the Law and the Prophets (5:39-40)

- Later, in 5:45-47, Jesus claims that Moses accuses his opponents. In a sense, Jesus seems to say that to understand Moses' message is to believe Jesus' claims to be God's special agent.

A SURPRISE PARTY

A crowd of people has been attracted to Jesus and his message, and they follow wherever he goes. Each of the four Gospels records a wondrous feeding of a crowd, and—except for the Passion narrative—this event is probably the most documented of the stories of Jesus. However, the story in John 6:5-14 is packed with unique features.

First and not surprisingly, John sets Jesus' passion in the context of the Passover celebration. The story of Israel's ancient redemption from the death penalty prepares us to think more deeply about the meaning of this feeding and particularly the meaning of Jesus' words in 6:25-71. The detail of the "great deal of grass" (6:10) emphasizes the season of the celebration. Later on, John's dating of Jesus' crucifixion will lead us to discuss why this Jewish festival was so important to the evangelist.

The little boy and his barley loaves and two little fish comprise the second unique feature of John's story of the meal for the multitude. Commentators have emphasized that barley loaves were the staple of the poorest of the poor in Palestine during Jesus' time. Of course, the disciples rightly ask what good could be served from such a meager portion.

The third unique feature is the mention that "when he [Jesus] had given thanks" (6:11), he had the food distributed. Matthew, Mark, and Luke record only that Jesus "blessed" the loaves and fishes. John's brief reference to Jesus essentially saying grace before the meal has sparked great discussion because of the Greek word translated as "given thanks." The word is *eucharisteō* (EU-KAW-RIS-TE-O), and it is one of the names the church came to use for Holy Communion or the Lord's Supper. Strangely enough, John has no mention of Jesus' last meal with the disciples, where he established what became the sacrament as we know it (Matthew 26:26-29; Mark 14:22-25; Luke 22:14-23). Therefore, some scholars argue that the feeding story in John 6 is actually John's version of the institution of the sacrament. An intriguing notion.

A fourth unique feature may seem minor. In the Synoptic Gospels, the disciples distribute the food to the crowd, but in John, Jesus himself distributes the food. This suggests a direct line between the gifts Jesus gives and those of us who receive them. Still another point in which John's story is unique involves Jesus' directions for the disciples to gather the leftovers so that none of them would be lost (6:12).

The conclusion of the feeding story allows the story line to continue well after the miracle meal. The crowd thinks they have witnessed a "sign" (and John does not dispute this), they conclude Jesus is a "prophet," and then they seek to force him to become their king (6:14-15). In John, Jesus is never at the mercy of human will; he determines his own destiny. By mentioning the crowd's efforts to enthrone Jesus, John gives this well-known story an element of suspense and surprise. Like a good drama, the plot moves along with only the slightest hints of its outcome.

AN AFTER-DINNER STROLL

Along with John 5:16-21, Matthew 14:22-33 and Mark 6:45-52 include a story of Jesus' walking on the water. However, Mark is the only one to link it with the feeding of the multitude as John does. The disciples are frightened by one of the sudden storms for which the Sea of Galilee was infamous. However, they are even more frightened by the sight of Jesus walking toward them. Jesus' response is the ominous "I am," which is translated in the NRSV as "It is I" (6:20). The disciples welcome their master into their boat, and immediately they end up on shore. John gives us two wonders for the price of one: Jesus walking on water and the mysterious landing of the disciples' boat.

CHANGING PARTNERS

Reader, beware: Don't get bogged down in trying to figure out the references to "the other side of the sea" in John 6:22-25. It's confusing, but the ensuing long discussion that begins at 6:25 and finally ends at 6:71 is the main point. One way of handling this extended conversation is by dividing it into sections according to whom Jesus is addressing.

The crowd (6:22-40)

The multitude present for the feeding miracle at the beginning of the chapter follows Jesus and finds him on the other side of the sea. Jesus immediately challenges their motives for seeking him out. They had come in hopes of getting still another meal—a free handout! He urges them to seek spiritual food, but they have no idea what he's talking about. They want him to bowl them over with some miraculous sign, but Jesus will have none of it. He compares himself with Moses and the gift of manna from heaven (Exodus 16) and contrasts it with the bread from his Father.

In John 6:35-40, Jesus makes a series of "I am" statements. In 6:35, he uses bread as a metaphor for the nourishment, sustenance, and energy that changes one's whole life. Then he shifts his emphasis to the question of how one comes to believe in him. In 6:37, he claims that God "gives" him those who believe and that he hangs on to them so that they cannot fall away and lose their relationship with God. The segment of the discussion in these verses concludes with Jesus' promise that "all who see the Son and believe in him may have eternal life; and I will raise them up on the last day" (6:40).

These verses introduce the issue of human freedom to believe and divine determination. In 6:37, for instance, believing is the decision of those who "come to" Jesus. But 6:37 suggests that God has determined who will believe. How much of the act of believing is our own decision, and how much is God's choosing? John sometimes stresses one and sometimes another. The point is that in John's Gospel, belief in Jesus is not presented as a simple matter of one's own decision.

The Jews (6:41-59)

Without explanation, Jesus changes conversation partners, and the Jews step forward. We are closest to the truth when we think of "the Jews" (at least in the way John uses the title) as the religious leaders of the day. Obviously they are distinct from the crowd that surely was comprised of people of Jewish commitment.

These new conversation partners are concerned about two matters. The first is Jesus' claim to be "the bread that came down from heaven," which becomes the theme of the discussion in 6:41-51. (In 6:52-58, the topic is Jesus' claim to give people "his flesh to eat.") His dialogue partners think they know where Jesus came from, and it is surely Joseph and his mother, not his "Father." Jesus often confuses his dialogue partners with statements they misunderstand.

Jesus is concerned to distinguish his gift to humans from all that God has been giving them throughout their history.

- God chooses some to be drawn to Jesus (6:44).

- But "everyone who has heard and learned from the Father comes to me" (6:45).

- Instead of the manna from heaven, which sustains people in their daily living, the "bread that comes down from heaven" gives people eternal life (6:48-50).

- The bread that Jesus gives "for the life of the world" is his flesh (6:51).

John 6:52 surfaces the second question the Jews have: "How can this man give us his flesh to eat?" Jesus proceeds now into the most difficult part of his message. He claims that the food he offers brings eternal life, and that food is his flesh and blood. Even more scandalous are the Greek terms Jesus uses in John to describe taking eternal life into oneself. When Jesus speaks in 6:53, he uses a form of an ordinary Greek word for "eat," *phagēte* (FA-GA-TE); but in 6:54, he uses the verb *trōgōn* (TRO-GON), a term most often used for the crude eating or munching of an animal, sometimes translated as "feed on." (The NRSV unfortunately translates both of those words in 6:53 and 6:54 as "eat" and loses the importance of the difference between them.) The point of this language is to drive home the importance of internalizing Christ and his message.

The disciples and the faithful (6:60-71)

Some of those who had been following Jesus were equally offended and scandalized by Jesus' words. This section and 20:24 are the only passages in

John in which the "twelve" are mentioned. Otherwise, all believers are referred to as disciples. If they wish, any and all of the disciples could withdraw and no longer follow Jesus, which is an important point. It is not just the divinely elected who are disciples. For that reason, Jesus invites them to separate themselves if they so desire.

Unlike the Synoptic Gospels, Peter is not given the honor of being the first one to declare Jesus' true identity (Matthew 16:13-20; Mark 8:27-30; Luke 9:18-21). However, in John he does confess, "Lord, to whom can we go? You have the words of eternal life" (6:68).

Disciple

Any believer and follower of Jesus. In John, it does not mean the inner circle of the twelve disciples. The numerical word seems reserved only for Jesus' chosen followers.

In the important conclusion to this long series of dialogues, Jesus affirms he has chosen each one of the disciples, even the one who will betray him (6:70-71). This is the first mention of the betrayer and the first of only three references to the devil in this Gospel (see 8:44 and 13:2 for the other two).

INVITATION TO DISCIPLESHIP

The first part of the invitation to discipleship in these readings is the summons to find indispensable health and nourishment in Christ. Jesus invites us to taste—to experience him—for ourselves. The implication is that when we take that taste, we find wholeness in our relationship with God and with a community of believers—a wholeness that entails body, mind, and spirit. Clearly, in John's Gospel, discipleship requires an overt act of feeding on God's love, grace, and presence, which can happen whenever we remember and reenact the Lord's Supper together.

As disciples of Christ, we join our voices with all those witnesses to the Jesus we find in John 6. Our lives are connected with the lives of all Christians. Discipleship is not a "lone-ranger" witness; rather, it is participating in a wide community of other witnesses, both present and past.

FOR REFLECTION

- Reflect on the man who was never able to get to the bubbling water in time to benefit from it. He was always squeezed out. When have you ever felt in competition with others who also are in need of Christ's healing? In those instances, what does John 5:1-9 say to you?

- In John 6:25-27, Jesus challenges the motivations of the crowd that has come across the lake to find him. How does Jesus challenge your motives for seeking him out? Suppose you had nothing to gain physically, financially, socially, or even eternally after death. Would you still follow Christ?

- In John 6:70, Jesus says to the faithful twelve disciples that he chose them for discipleship. What are the risks and benefits of knowing God has picked you to be a disciple?

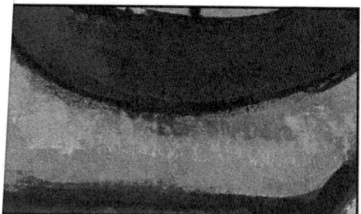

EFLECTION

...mmentary about Jesus' rejec-

...r enemy because he threat-
...very perception of reality.
...ense of an entire system of
...e rejection of Jesus in this
... of new and unprecedented
...ife of faith.... The contem-
...side the church. The con-
...ext to examine when and by
...nowledge of God brought by
...ging to existing religious sys-
...pel of John: Introduction,
...il R. O'Day, in *The New*
Interpreter's B... ...*e Volumes*, Vol. IX, edited by
Leander E. Keck [Abingdon Press, 1995]; page 581.)

Where in your church life do you see Christians implicitly rejecting Jesus' message because it threatens their power and position? How is it that our "religious systems and structures" weaken God's word for us in Christ? When have *we* shied away from the truth of Christ's revelation because we feared for our own power and position? What can you do to witness *within* the church to allow the gospel message to remake our institutional life?

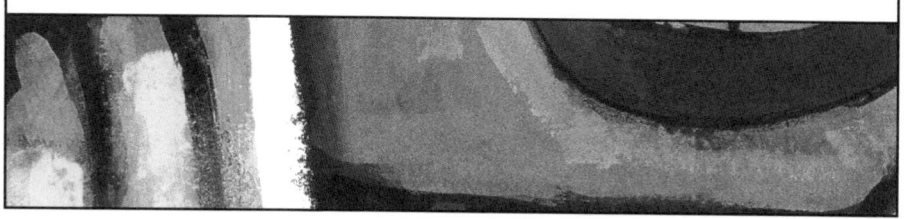

To Believe or Not to Believe

There was considerable complaining about him among the crowds. While some were saying, "He is a good man," others were saying, "No, he is deceiving the crowd."

—John 7:12

INTRODUCTION

Many of us feel swamped with invitations to believe this or that religious claim. Witnesses come to our front door and invite us to believe as they believe. Television preachers persistently want us to believe as they do and sometimes warn us of the dangers of not believing. Some say that the terrible natural calamities in our world are acts of God to punish some for not believing! Moreover, these days the invitations to believe are multiplied by the presence of other world religious traditions as well as numerous sectarian groups.

So, we find ourselves asking over and over again whether we should believe or not believe. We don't want to believe the claims that are not true, but neither do we want to miss an opportunity to believe what is true! Some of those who encountered Jesus were faced with that same dilemma.

DAILY ASSIGNMENTS

DAY ONE: John 7:1-36

In these verses, Jesus is at the Feast of the Tabernacles in Jerusalem, where he encounters opposition from the residents of Judea. To gain some knowledge of this feast (also called the Festival of Booths), read Leviticus 23:34-43; Deuteronomy 16:13-17; and Nehemiah 8:14-18. What do you think of Jesus' brothers in these verses? Are they his opponents or just misunderstanding inquirers? Why is Jesus presented as a kind of elusive figure in 7:11-13? Why is it that the leaders seek to arrest him already?

"Show yourself to the world"

They don't believe he is the Messiah

DAY TWO: John 7:37-52

In addition to the passages in John, read Proverbs 18:4; Isaiah 55:11; Ezekiel 47:1-11; and Zechariah 14:8. How do the Old Testament texts relate to Jesus' statement in 7:37-39? What does John 7:37-39 mean, and why does Jesus cause such a division among the people? How should we interpret Nicodemus and his words in 7:50-52? Has he become a believer or not?

Living water = holy spirit

People wanted to believe him but could not understand how the Messiah could not come from Bethlehem.

Yes —

DAY THREE: John 7:53–8:11

Before reading the story of Jesus and the woman caught in adultery, read Leviticus 20:10; Deuteronomy 22:13-24; and Ezekiel 16:38-40. Reflect on how we practice Christian forgiveness and reconciliation without empowering the evil impulses in some people. What does Jesus' admonition, "Go your way, and from now on do not sin again" (8:11), say about John's view of second chances and judgment?

He did not condemn her but also did not condone sin → forgiveness

DAY FOUR: John 8:12-30

With Jesus' claim to be the "light of the world" (8:12) in mind, read Exodus 13:17-22 and Wisdom of Solomon 18:3-4 (in the Apocrypha). How do these references to light help us understand what is meant by Jesus' statement that he is the light?

God led the Israelites at a pillar of cloud by day & pillar of fire by night

Jesus is light that leads us to God

DAY FIVE: John 8:31-59

This is a passage often cited to condemn the Jewish people, and Jesus' words to the religious leaders are taken to be brutal and devastating but true. How can we read this without generalizing about all the Jewish people? What difference does it make that the discussion in this passage is prefaced by the remark in 8:30, indicating that many of the Jews believe in Jesus?

DAY SIX:

Read the commentary in the participant book.

TENTING TIME AT THE TEMPLE

Tension mounts as Jesus is about to go to Jerusalem. The Festival of Booths (or Feast of the Tabernacles) was an agricultural celebration when people gathered outside their vineyards and lived there for seven or eight days in huts. It commemorated the time the people of Israel wandered in the wilderness and lived in temporary shelters.

Chronos and Kairos

Jesus responds to his brothers' request by declaring that his "time" has not yet come (7:6). The Greek language used in Jesus' day had two words for time. The term *chronos* (KRO-NOS), seen in the word *chronology*, has to do with what might be called "clock time." The other term is *kairos* (KI-ROS) and was used to designate what might be called "crucial time." The word John uses to record Jesus' response to his brothers in John 7:6 is *kairos*.

Jesus will not allow even his brothers to manipulate his actions (John 7:3-9). They have demonstrated their unbelief and aroused Jesus' distrust. Judea had established itself as the home of the religious leaders who were seeking to kill Jesus. Note that "the Jews" are in Judea. Obviously "Jews" refers to the religious leaders and not all Jews. The Judeans generally tended to feel superior to Galileans since the latter were in more immediate contact with non-Jewish neighbors and were regarded as unclean.

As we have seen, Jesus is not about to be controlled. Despite opposition, he goes to Jerusalem. There, he causes a division among the people, as he often does (7:11-13). Jesus refuses to take credit for his teachings and attributes everything he says to God. However, he is puzzled by the efforts of followers of Moses to arrest and kill him (7:19).

Matthew, Mark, and Luke all report that Jesus cast demons out of afflicted persons. In contrast, John includes no stories of Jesus' calling demons out of people. As agents of Satan, demons were believed to cause the loss of mental capacities, and Jesus' opponents interpret his statement that some are trying to kill him as some kind of demonic martyr complex.

WHERE DID YOU COME FROM?

John 7:26 introduces the question of whether or not Jesus is indeed the long-awaited Messiah. Tradition taught that no one would know where the Messiah would come from, but "some of the people of Jerusalem" (7:25) were pretty sure they knew Jesus came from Nazareth. Thus, as a Galilean in Judea, Jesus is rejected outright on the basis of his earthly background. In fact, as he will argue himself, Jesus comes from above, from God who sent him into the world. This accounts for Jesus' declaration—when some try to arrest him—that his opponents cannot come to where he is going (7:32-34). His opponents, of course, misunderstand and think that Jesus is planning to go into the Greco-Roman world and teach the Greeks. What the Jews in the passage call "the Dispersion" refers to those Jews who lived outside of Jerusalem. Ironically this misunderstanding contains an element of truth: The church will later go throughout the known world and win Greeks to its faith (John 12:20-21).

Within this context of opposition and hostility, another problematic topic arises in John 7:37. Having earlier claimed to the Samaritan woman that he is living water, here he once again claims to be the source of water, this time crying out to all within earshot. But look carefully at what he says in 7:38: Is Jesus the source of the water, or is the believer the source? Note what Scripture Jesus quotes. Some argue that Jesus is the source of water, some say it is the believer, and some say the statement is intentionally ambiguous because the water flows from both Christ and believers. The Scripture Jesus quotes comes from Proverbs 18:4; Isaiah 55:11; Ezekiel 47:1-11; Zechariah 14:8—or it may be a combination of themes from a number of these passages. John seems to interpret these words as having to do with the Spirit Jesus gives the disciples in 20:22. In this case, water represents the Spirit, and the issues of the conflict between Jesus and the religious leaders will be resolved only through the gift of the Spirit. Christ's disciples, then, may be the means by which God's Spirit enters the lives of others and strengthens the relationships among humans.

The seventh chapter of John makes clear the division between those who believed Jesus might be the Messiah and those who did not. The question of Jesus' origins continues to be a source of contention in 7:40-44, this time with regard to his birth. Jesus comes from Galilee, while Scripture claims the Messiah will be a descendant of David, born in Bethlehem (Micah 5:2). For many Jews in Jesus' day, the issue of where Jesus came from determined his identity.

John 7 concludes with the report of a meeting of the religious leaders in response to the ruckus Jesus has been causing (7:45-52). The police lack courage to arrest someone who impresses them so. The authorities respond that no one has believed Jesus except the "crowd," who know nothing about the Law. The common folk did not have time for or interest in a detailed pursuit of the Law, as did the Pharisees and other religious leaders. Consequently, they were deemed unworthy of judging the truthfulness of Jesus' statements.

Then, our old friend Nicodemus makes a surprise appearance and challenges the appropriateness of judging Jesus without allowing him a chance to defend himself. His suggestion is met with accusations that Nicodemus is a Galilean and claims that no prophet could arise from Galilee. Has Nicodemus become a secret follower—or at least an admirer—of Jesus?

Hostility toward Jesus is palpable throughout these readings. He is misunderstood, judged, and condemned by a host of opponents offering snapshots of a "know-it-all" religiosity that was stubbornly closed to new possibilities. Part of any invitation to follow Jesus entails avoiding the kind of arrogance and self-righteousness that refuses to consider any fresh insights into faith.

ON THROWING STONES AND WRITING IN THE DIRT

The story of the woman charged with adultery in John 7:53–8:11 is not found in the earliest and most important manuscripts of John. It first appears in a Greek text dated about 900 A.D. Scholars have long argued that the passage is a later insertion into John, and some even think the style in which it is written is not like that of John. The long history of uncertainty about this story accounts for why many Bibles print it framed within brackets and accompanied by an explanatory note.

Notwithstanding the questions raised by this little story, it has won the hearts of many readers and represents a Jesus figure common to the Gospels. This is the only time we hear of the "scribes" in John, but they make frequent appearances in the other Gospels. These scribes transcribed the Scriptures and hence were regarded as experts in their interpretation. According to Jewish law, if a married woman had sexual intercourse with another man other than her husband, she was guilty of adultery, and the common punishment of such an offense was stoning (Leviticus 20:10; Deuteronomy 22:22; Ezekiel 16:38-40). Clearly meaning to trap Jesus, the crowd asks Jesus what he thinks should be done with her. Jesus responds by remaining silent and writing something in the dirt.

What exactly did Jesus write in the dirt that day? The question has stirred the imagination of nearly every reader of the story. However, those who remembered and transmitted the story did not seem to think what Jesus wrote was important, so we need not overly concern ourselves with it. Instead, we would do well to pay attention to Jesus' next words, for they provide us with the heart of the story. He invites anyone in the crowd who is not guilty of sin to start throwing stones and then returns to his writing. After what was likely an uncomfortable pause, one by one, those gathered around the woman realize that Jesus' invitation is not to begin the woman's execution but to begin their own self-examination. They walk away. Then Jesus speaks to the woman, having already demonstrated to her that no one can claim enough moral purity to execute her. Jesus admonishes her to go her way and sin no more.

As widely known as this story is, we might think that condemnation of others would be rare among those who claim membership among the religious and the righteous—but it is not. The story forces us to acknowledge that no one can claim so high a moral ground as to stand in judgment of others' sinfulness. Jesus practices a forgiveness that assaults even time-honored religious statutes. Jesus calls for his disciples to acknowledge first that they have no business throwing stones.

WHAT TIME IS IT?

Because of the intrusion of the story of the woman, we are not sure to whom Jesus is speaking in 8:12-30. When he says he is the "light of the world," Jesus employs one of John's favorite literary devices: dualism, or the use of a pair of words that are opposites, like light and darkness. In nearly every case in the Gospel, one of the words in the pair expresses life lived *out* of relationship with God, and the other word expresses life lived *in* relationship with God. Generally, John views right and wrong as diametrically opposed and irreconcilable, so his choice of these word pairs supports that view.

Jesus' claim that he is the light of the world is especially appropriate on the occasion of the Feast of the Tabernacles (recall Exodus 13:21-22 and the Wisdom of Solomon 18:3-4). The issue of witnesses arises again along with the charge that Jesus cannot testify in his own behalf (see John 5:30-47). But who is fit to judge? According to 8:15-19, the central theme is that God alone is both judge and witness. According to Numbers 35:30 and Deuteronomy 17:6, two witnesses are required to sentence a person to death. Jesus says his role is not to convict anyone, but if it is necessary, his judgment is God's. The accusers then try to corner Jesus by asking where his Father is (8:19). God is his Father. If we ask where we find God, the Christian answer is in the incarnation of the divine Word, in Jesus of Nazareth. As readers begin to wonder when this mysterious "hour" will occur (8:20), the narrative becomes more and more suspenseful. (Compare 2:4 and 12:23.)

The topic of the future hour entails Jesus' "going away" (8:21)—that is, his death on the cross. When he announces that he will go away, the crowd's misunderstandings are almost humorous. Some wonder if he will kill himself (see also 14:28 and 16:17). Ironically, his going away does entail his death, and a voluntary death at that.

The harshness of Jesus' words in 8:21—"you will die in your sin"—cannot be avoided. The consequences of being without Christ are serious. However, note that the word *sin* here is in the singular, so it does not refer to sundry minor offenses. In John, as elsewhere in the New Testament, *sin* in the singular means the results of living outside a relationship with God. However, in 8:24, unbelief expresses itself in numerous specific offenses, which are called "sins" (in the plural).

The crucial point for John in these verses is that his readers believe that Jesus is indeed the great "I am"—God's own self (8:24). However, those who are listening to Jesus speak want him to say more than simply "I am." They just don't get it. They want Jesus to declare precisely who or what he is. And after his response, the puzzled crowd asks Jesus again, "Who are you?" (8:25). Jesus then says that only after they have lifted him up will they understand what he means by saying "I am." (In 8:24 and 8:28, "I am" is translated as "I am he.") Once Jesus further declares that the "one who sent" him is always with him, John notes that "many believed in him" (8:29-30).

OUT OF WHOM?

Beginning in 8:31, much of Jesus' next conversation pivots around one question: From whom does Jesus come? The conversation is sparked by Jesus' promise that by believing in him, listeners will be freed. Those around Jesus are offended and insist that as descendants of Abraham, they have never been enslaved (8:33). This is obviously an exaggeration, for the Jews knew one oppressor after another—first Egyptian, then Persian, and now Roman. However, Jesus is speaking of the "spiritual freedom" of which we are robbed by our alienation from our Creator (that is, because of sin). He then contrasts the roles of a slave and a child within a family (8:34-36). There is a play on the word *son* in this passage. Jesus is God's "Son," in the sense of sharing the divine family. Hence, only Christ has the power to free humans from the bondage of their isolation from God.

If the religious leaders were true descendants of Abraham, they would not seek to kill Jesus. However, they insist they are *ek* (meaning "out of," "originating from") Abraham (8:39-41). Yet, by seeking to kill Jesus, they are doing what their "father does." That is, as Jesus plainly states, their father must be the devil! (8:44). They protest that they are not illegitimate children but true children of God. Not so, declares Jesus: "Whoever is from [*ek*] God hears the words of God" (8:47). We reveal our true origin in how we respond to Christ.

When Jesus affirms that anyone who believes in him will never die, his opponents' anger intensifies even more. Why, then, did Abraham and the prophets die? Jesus counters by saying he knows God and keeps God's word, and Abraham sees and rejoices in him. How could Jesus, who is not yet fifty, claim to have seen Abraham? He declares that he existed before Abraham did—notice the "I am" again—an outrageous claim. He would surely have been stoned had he not hidden himself and left the temple (8:51-59).

INVITATION TO DISCIPLESHIP

Who is the source of being from whom we derive our identity? Religious tradition is not enough. It is not enough to say, for example, "I came out of John Wesley or Martin Luther or John Calvin." The question of our *ek* is more basic. Our discipleship necessitates that day by day we ask, "Whose we are?" It is not enough to ask and answer the question once. In our confusing world, we as Christian believers need to deal continuously with that question.

FOR REFLECTION

- There are times when being a follower of Jesus is neither popular nor easy. Where in your life right now do you struggle with opposition to something you regard as essential to your Christian faith? What can you do about it?

- Recall the metaphors Jesus used to express his mission: "the light of the world," "the bread of life," "living water," and so forth. Think about your own faith and discipleship, and imagine a metaphor like the ones in John that expresses your faith. What picture of Christ and God's love summarizes what you believe and practice?

- To what degree does Christian faith develop as a result of our family of origin? How can we recognize the importance of our roots without then minimizing our human freedom to believe or not to believe?

- Jesus' words are often misunderstood by his listeners. What are some of the teachings of Jesus you have trouble understanding?

FOR FURTHER REFLECTION

The dialogue between Jesus and the Jews in John 8:31-59 contains some of the harshest and most insulting words about Jews and Judaism to be found in Christian literature. Jesus is said to have declared that his Jewish listeners are not children of Abraham but rather children of "your father the devil" (8:44). In effect, he "demonizes" the Jews, making them agents of evil.

How do you respond to the attack on the Jews in the Gospel of John? How have you experienced Jews and Judaism? Since John is part of our Bible, how can we refute this view without compromising our belief in the Bible? Is it enough to argue that John's anti-Jewish perspective is only a reflection of the historical setting for the writing of the Gospel? How would you explain the harsh words of John about the Jews to a Christian trying to understand John's Gospel?

Are We Blind?

When he [Jesus] had said this, he spat on the ground and made mud with the saliva and spread the mud on the [blind] man's eyes.... Then he went and washed and came back able to see.

—John 9:6-7

INTRODUCTION

Since I was tall for my age, I started playing basketball when I was in the eighth grade. I soon learned something disturbing, however. I could not see the scoreboard. So, I would run down the court next to a teammate and ask him what the score was. Another friend and I frequently went to movies together. He got glasses to overcome his nearsightedness. One day, I decided to ask him to allow me to look at the screen through his glasses. Wow, I could see so much better with his glasses! As it turned out, I was drastically nearsighted. When I finally had my eyes tested and put on my first pair of glasses, it was like seeing a whole new world. To this day, I have a keen sensitivity to those who are visually challenged. The story of how I came to get glasses reminds me of how easy it can be, as Christians, to overlook our spiritual blindness. It may not be a bad idea every so often to ask the question "Surely we are not blind, are we?"

DAILY ASSIGNMENTS

DAY ONE: John 9:1-17

After reading the John passage, read Mark 8:22-26. Note the similarities and differences between John's and Mark's accounts. The exchange between Jesus and his disciples in John 9:2-3 reflects an understanding supported by Exodus 20:5. How is that understanding still operative today? How do you react to the notion that in some cases God "causes" an illness as an opportunity to reveal the power of divine healing? Read 1 Kings 17:17-24 and 2 Kings 4:8-37, and compare Elijah and Elisha's wonders with Jesus' healing of the blind man.

DAY TWO: John 9:18-34

Here we have a head-to-head collision between the religious authorities (called "the Jews") and the man healed of blindness. Note all the reasons the religious authorities give to explain away the blind man's healing. How does the healed man respond? What do we learn from this confrontation about our own discipleship? Why do you think the healed man remains so fearless in the face of religious authorities?

DAY THREE: John 9:35-41

John 9:35 is one of the places where John has Jesus speak of himself as the "Son of Man." John seems to favor the titles *Son of God* and simply *Son*. Read John 1:51; 3:13, 14; 5:27; 6:27, 53, 62; 8:28; 12:23; and 13:31. Now read Daniel 7:13-14 (note that the NRSV uses the term *human being* instead of *son of man*). What do you think "Son of Man" means when applied to Jesus in John's Gospel? What's to keep us from thinking that the healed man has simply been overpowered by Jesus' miracle and believes only because of it? What does John 9:39 mean? Read Isaiah 6:10; 29:18; 35:5; 42:7, 18-19; and Psalm 146:8. How do you think these passages help us understand John 9:39?

DAY FOUR: John 10:1-18

Have someone read these verses aloud while you close your eyes and listen. Then talk with your reader to compare what mental images were evoked by the text. How did this exercise help you understand the language of the passage and its message? Compare the following passages with John 10:1-18: Psalm 23; Isaiah 40:10-11; Jeremiah 23:1-6; Ezekiel 34:1-16, 23-24; Zechariah 11:4-17; and Luke 15:1-7.

DAY FIVE: John 10:19-42

The setting for most of these readings is the Festival of the Dedication. Read Daniel 9:24-27 and Matthew 24:15 for some background. Go back and reread John 3:17-36; 5:24; and 6:35-47. What do you think these passages teach about believing (or not believing) that Jesus is who he says he is?

DAY SIX:

Read the commentary in the participant book.

HERE'S MUD IN YOUR EYE

Have you ever gotten something in your eyes to the extent that you could hardly bear the pain of opening them? In John 9:1-12, Jesus heals blindness using mud made with his own saliva (unlike in Mark 8:22-26, where Jesus heals with spittle alone). Like many of the healing stories in John, this one involves a drastically needy subject. The man was born blind, and that fact sparks the disciples' question as to whose sin caused his illness. The disciples' question arises from passages like Exodus 20:5: "You shall not bow down to them or worship them; for I the LORD your God am a jealous God, punishing children for the iniquity of parents, to the third and the fourth generation of those who reject me." Jesus responds that the man's parents are not responsible for their son's condition, but then he offers an even more disturbing perspective: that blindness overcame this man in order that Jesus might heal him and thereby reveal "God's works" (John 9:3). Some commentators have argued that the statement does not offer a cause-and-effect relationship but only suggests that the man's blindness is an occasion for God's healing work. Yet Jesus' words are here before us, so we are left to work out our own understanding of God's part in human illness and divine healing.

Jesus sends the man to wash in the pool known as "Sent." The waters wash away the mud and the blindness, and for the first time in his life, the man can see. Earlier in John 8:12, Jesus declared himself to be the "light of the world"; now he brings light to a blind man's eyes. Reaction to the man's healing is mixed and swift. Some are ready to acknowledge it, but others argue that this is a different person. Sometimes we are hesitant to credit certain events to God, and other times we are too eager to do so! They ask the healed man where Jesus has gone, but he does not know. All he knows is that he can see.

CRIME SCENE INVESTIGATION

A blind man can now see. What an occasion for joy, it would seem. But the Pharisees are not happy; they are upset because a sabbath law had been broken. The interpretation of the third commandment—to keep the sabbath day "holy" (Exodus 31:14)—was still developing in Jesus' time but generally forbade healing on the sabbath except when the patient's life was endangered. Once again Jesus finds himself in conflict with the religious leaders, most especially the Pharisees, the ones most zealous in observing the Law.

Notice how the religious leaders in this story split in their attitude toward Jesus (9:16). One group argues that a sinner (one who violates the Law) could not perform such wonders as this. The question in their minds is "Where does Jesus come from? Does he come from God?" The blind man thinks Jesus is surely a prophet. Foremost in his mind might have been the stories of Elijah and Elisha, extraordinary wonder-workers in the Hebrew Scriptures (1 Kings 17:17-24; 2 Kings 4:8-37). John doesn't record the Pharisees even giving him the benefit of a response.

In any case, the leaders (called "the Jews" in John) move immediately to the next phase of their investigation. Had the man really been blind before he encountered Jesus? Was the healing a "sleight-of-hand" stunt? Off they go to question the man's parents. But Mom and Dad can only point the investigators to their son. Understandably the parents are terrified of the religious leaders because "the Jews had already agreed that anyone who confessed Jesus to be the Messiah would be put out of the synagogue" (9:22; see also John 16:2). It is conceivable that John was deliberately addressing Jewish Christians here in the midst of a struggle between the church and synagogue.

Put Out of the Synagogue

We find the Greek word for being "put out of the synagogue" (*aposynagōgos*, AP-AH-SUN-AGO-GOS) in three places in John: 9:22; 12:42; and 16:2. It is the basis of a hypothesis that John was written soon after the Christians were expelled from the synagogue. This hypothesis gained a significant following among scholars. While it fashioned a believable picture of the situation when John wrote, it is speculative and may or may not be true.

CROSS-EXAMINATION

The blind man is of little help. When the leaders try to get more information about Jesus out of him, he is noncommittal. He is not about to sell Jesus out to win favor with the establishment. All he claims is that once he was blind and now he sees. He even taunts the leaders by asking if they're seeking to follow Jesus themselves. The leaders recoil at such a remark. They claim allegiance to Moses—at least they are sure where he comes from, which is more than they can say for Jesus (7:27)

The blind man pushes his interviewers even harder. How could they not account for someone who cured a man blind from birth (9:31-33)? However, the leaders are not about to be instructed by the offspring of sinners, and they run him off. They obviously believe he was born blind because his parents were sinful. This blind man provides us with a portrait of someone whose encounter with Jesus emboldens him to challenge the powers of his own religious establishment. There may be times when even we as Christians today will need to muster such boldness.

A CONFIRMATION SERVICE

When Jesus and the blind man meet again, Jesus asks him to confess his faith openly. The man is anxious to believe but still needs to know who the Son of Man is. Having heard Jesus explicitly identify himself as the "Son of Man" (in this case, a title for the Messiah), the man is eager to confess his faith: "Lord, I believe" (9:38).

The verses following the blind man's confession (9:39-41) are a preview of what is to come in the next chapter. But it also seems clear that John wants his readers to hear their own concerns and issues in the responses of the Pharisees to Jesus' words. Notice that 9:39 uses the language of seeing and becoming blind, and the Pharisees (who are eavesdropping on the conversation) think Jesus is talking about them. Jesus defines their sin not as blindness but as denial that they are guilty. Those who protest their innocence the loudest often turn out to be the guilty ones. Then we hear the religious leaders asking incredulously, "Surely we are not blind, are we?" (9:40). Are we? Discipleship in John's Gospel can mean not denying that we are blind too.

FOLLOW THE LEADER

As they stand nearby, Jesus' opponents hear his speech in John 10, words clearly intended—at least in part—for them. What Jesus says in this chapter is like a kaleidoscope turning again and again to reveal a colorful new word picture. Each picture is designed to suggest one more layer of meaning based on the person, actions, and environment of the simple shepherd.

The kaleidoscope turns first to highlight the picture of the sheepfold and those who avoid the entrance, whom the text calls thieves and bandits. They are contrasted with the shepherd, who enters the sheepfold legitimately by the door. In first-century Judea, the sheepfold was a simple structure made of stones arranged to form a crude wall within which the sheep were held. The picture immediately moves to the intimate relationship between the shepherd and the sheep. They trust and follow the shepherd because they recognize the shepherd's voice, but not the voice of a stranger.

IS JESUS A GATE OR A SHEPHERD?

The kaleidoscope turns again, abruptly changing from the image of Jesus as "the shepherd of the sheep" (10:2) to "the gate for the sheep" (10:7). We are forced to shift our images of Jesus from a shepherd to an entranceway. Some try to reconcile these two different pictures by suggesting that at night the shepherd would stretch out across the entrance and sleep there. While such an attempt is certainly noteworthy, it is preferable simply to consider this new picture on its own merit. It makes perfect sense that Jesus would want the image of the gate linked to his declaration that he is the way to salvation, to "pasture." The metaphor of the pastures represents a meaningful and peaceful life, what Jesus calls abundant life (that is, abundance of quality, not necessarily quantity) in 10:10. The identity of the "thief" in that same verse is unclear, except for the proximity of this passage to the conflict with religious leaders in John 9. The whole of the passage bombards our imaginations with shifting and differing images focused on the sheep, sheepfolds, and shepherd themes. Jesus does not so much mix his metaphors here as he holds our attention while he turns the kaleidoscope from one rich image to another.

> **Very Truly**
>
> The NRSV translation of the Greek *amen, amen.* It is little more than an implicit declaration that what follows is of the highest importance. It has the sense of the supreme affirmation.

The distinction between the shepherd, the owner of the sheep, and the hired hand complicates the metaphor even more. (See Isaiah 40:10-11; Jeremiah 23:1-6; Ezekiel 34:1-16, 23-24; and Zechariah 11:4-17.) John 10:11 begins to prepare us for the Passion story in the final chapters. "Lays down his life" means

Jesus *voluntarily gives up* his life for the sake of the world, as is repeated in 10:15, 17-18. (See the use of the expression in 13:37, 38; and 15:13.)

Jesus' absolute care for the welfare of humans is contrasted with the hired hand's lack of care. These hired hands, thieves, and bandits run in the presence of danger and try to save their own necks. These figures appear to refer to the religious leaders, who are pictured as so absorbed in their own agendas that they lose touch with the common people. Such an image is an appropriate warning for the contemporary church.

Once again, Jesus expands and deepens the imagery. Like a good shepherd, Jesus knows his sheep, and they know him. In this context, *know* probably means more than intellectual knowledge or recognition of others. It is the deepest sort of relationship. The Hebrew word for "know" is *yadah* (YA-DAH), a term that means intimacy, so that the verb form could be used for the intimate act of sexual intercourse (see Genesis 4:1).

In 10:16, Jesus refers to "other sheep." Who exactly are these other sheep? The most common explanation is that they are the Gentiles (or non-Jews) of the Greco-Roman world. If we take that meaning, then the "one flock, one shepherd" of 10:16 is probably John's metaphor for the one worldwide community of Christian believers. In other words, we are among these "other sheep."

This section of John (10:17-18) closes the series of metaphors with reference to God's love of Jesus and emphasizes that Jesus' death is voluntary. It is worth noting that in John's Gospel, *Jesus is never forced to do anything.* John makes absolutely clear that the Father's will for the Son is above human will, and nothing will distract the Son from fulfilling the Father's mission in the world.

However, the Messiah's presence in the world does create a chasm between those who believe and those who do not. John also makes clear that Christ is a controversial character. He elicits one of two extreme responses—belief or unbelief. There is no sitting on the fence. Either commit to God's love in Christ or join forces to repress that love. In our complicated world, the search for the "middle way" seems the only way. However, when it comes to the kind of God we follow, there are only two ways to go, and no path in between.

DEEPER TROUBLE

Beginning with John 10:22, John deliberately locates Jesus in a particular time and place as he continues explaining who he is. The time is the Festival of the Dedication, or better known today as "Hanukkah." It celebrates the success of the Jewish revolt against Syrian oppression and the establishment of a new altar to replace the one polluted by the oppressors around 164 B.C. (See Daniel 9:27 and Matthew 24:15.) The place is a *portico* (one of the covered areas surrounding the Temple), where Jesus is once again interrogated by a none-too-friendly crowd of Jewish leaders. However, their question is a good one: Are you or are you not the Messiah? Jesus claims he has told them already and his deeds point to the truth, but they still won't believe because they "do not belong to my sheep" (10:26). His sheep know his voice and follow him. As we have seen, John sometimes sounds as if some are destined to accept Christ and others to reject him. (See also 3:18-36; 5:24; 6:35-47; 11:49-52; 12:24; 19:10.) Christian interpreters over the centuries have handled the issue of divine determinism in different ways.

Jesus answers further in 10:27-30, asserting that he gives "eternal life" (that is, true, authentic life) to *those whom God has given him.* They cannot be torn away from God. In the early manuscripts of John, there are a number of differences as to the exact wording of 10:29. The major question is, what is greater? Is what the Father has given greater, or is God greater? But the next verse is more important and perhaps more problematic: "The Father and I are one." This statement, along with others similar to it, has shaped the church's doctrine of the Trinity and has been crucial to Christians' understanding of Christ. What exactly does being "one" mean? Traditionally, Christians have believed that God and Christ form a single identity and are one in "substance." Others have suggested that the oneness is the unity of love, will, and commitment. However it is understood, the question remains one to struggle over.

The Jews who heard Jesus speak were not impressed or convinced. John tells us that "they took up stones again to stone him" (10:31). Stoning was saved for those who profaned the Law in some way, and members of the crowd interpret Jesus' words as blasphemous. While we have little knowledge of what exactly constituted blasphemy in first-century Judaism, 10:33 suggests that it occurs anytime a human tries to make her or himself God (see Mark 2:7). We have no historical evidence that stoning was the punishment for such statements, but the action of the crowd seems understandable, given what they had heard Jesus say.

As a good rabbi of the time might have done, Jesus defends himself by citing Scripture, in this case Psalm 82:6. The argument is a familiar formula of "if this, then that": *If* (in the words of the psalm) God calls humans "gods," *then* Jesus is right in calling himself God, since God has sent him into the world. In 10:37-38 Jesus shifts the subject to his "works." If he does the works of God, then the Jews should believe them and believe Jesus was sent from God.

The crowd is still not convinced and tries to arrest him. But Jesus slips away, as he customarily does. He crosses the Jordan and ends up in "Bethany across the Jordan" (see 1:28). This is not the Bethany near Jerusalem where Lazarus, Mary, and Martha lived (11:1) but rather a location that is lost to us today. Wherever it was, the people there believe in him, and the chapter closes on a positive note.

INVITATION TO DISCIPLESHIP

How we follow Jesus invariably has its roots in how we understand Jesus. And though discipleship is not simply a matter of getting our theology right, it is a matter of trusting that Jesus rightly reveals the character of God. Like those who listened to Jesus in Jerusalem, it is easy to question the truthfulness of Jesus' message. Too often skepticism is easier than belief. In fact, if we read carefully, we see that Jesus' opponents are not so different than we are. We need to ask ourselves whether or not we too are blinded by the darkness of the world.

FOR REFLECTION

- How would you describe the personality of the man born blind in John 9? What must his life have been like when he was blind? What do you suppose this man went on to do after his healing?

- Imagine you are having a serious conversation with a person who does not accept the Christian message. How could your understanding of what Jesus says in John 10 help you form your thoughts? Where would you begin? What would be your goals for the conversation?

- Read 1 Maccabees 4:36-59 (from the Apocrypha section in your study Bible). What relation do you see between the story of the rededication of the Temple and Jesus' words in John 10:22-42?

- Why would you say some of the Pharisees were so resistant to Jesus' message? What about Jesus repelled those so observant of the Jewish law?

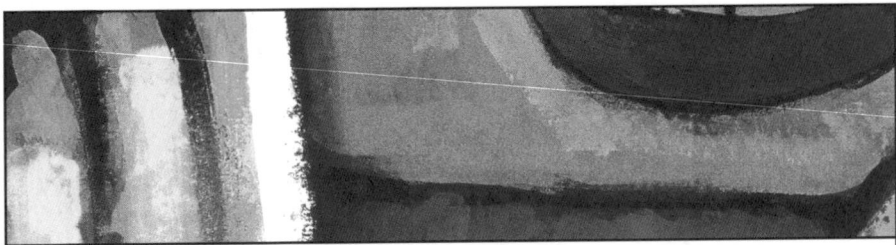

FOR FURTHER REFLECTION

Shepherds have been romanticized in the modern world and especially in the church. However, the more we learn about life in Palestine at the time of Jesus, the more we realize that shepherds were not the noble characters we have made them out to be. In his commentary on Luke 15:3-7, R. Alan Culpepper writes these instructive words:

> In contrast to the positive image of the shepherd in both the OT and NT writings, shepherds had acquired a bad reputation by the first century as shiftless, thieving, trespassing hirelings. Shepherding was listed among the despised trades by the rabbis, along with camel drivers, sailors, gamblers with dice, dyers, and tax collectors. (From "The Gospel of Luke: Introduction, Commentary, and Reflections," by R. Alan Culpepper, in *The New Interpreter's Bible: A Commentary in Twelve Volumes*, Vol. IX, edited by Leander E. Keck [Abingdon Press, 1995]; page 296.)

Shepherds had earned their bad reputation in part by their behavior in the villages of Palestine. They would bed their sheep just outside a village, and then after sunset they would sneak into the village and steal as much as they could. By the time the villagers awakened the next morning, the shepherds had taken their flocks and moved on to another site. Yet Jesus chose to use the shepherd as a metaphor for his own ministry.

How does this view of the shepherd affect your reading of John 10:1-18? Imagine how the first readers of John might have felt about Jesus picturing himself as a shepherd.

I Couldn't Believe My Eyes!

Many...who had come with Mary and had seen what Jesus did, believed in him. But some of them went to the Pharisees and told them what he had done.

—John 11:45-46

INTRODUCTION

Some years ago we were touring the national parks in the southwestern United States when we saw some scenery that was simply unbelievable. Again and again we would rub our eyes to be sure we were not being misled by a hallucination. That beautiful scenery made us question our vision!

Similarly, most of us could recall a location or an event or a scene that prompted us to declare, "I can't believe my eyes." What we saw or what we experienced may have seemed so strange that we couldn't immediately comprehend it. In some sense, the chapters in John we are about to study are about believing or not believing our eyes.

DAILY ASSIGNMENTS

DAY ONE: John 11:1-16

What do you make of the fact that Lazarus, who is not mentioned in the Gospel until John 11, is referred to as "he whom you [Jesus] love" (11:3)? Why does Jesus delay in going to Bethany? How does the delay affect the narrative? How does the fact that Jesus says Lazarus is asleep affect the importance of Jesus' "raising" him from the tomb? Read Jeremiah 13:16 and compare it with John 11:9-10. Why does Thomas think they are going to die with Jesus (11:16)?

DAY TWO: John 11:17-44

What does Martha mean in 11:21? What does Jesus mean in 11:25-26 by first saying that believers live after death and then that believers "will never die"? Why is Jesus so distressed in 11:33-35 when he surely knows he will raise Lazarus from the tomb? How does the role of the "Jews" in this story (for instance, 11:31) relate to the negative portrayal of the Jews earlier in the Gospel?

DAY THREE: John 11:45-57

How do you understand 11:48 and the fear that Jesus' signs will result in the Romans destroying the nation? What is your reaction to the words of Caiaphas in 11:49-50? What kind of suspense does 11:57 create in the story?

DAY FOUR: John 12:1-19

For the background of Jesus' entry into Jerusalem, read Psalm 118:25-26 and Zechariah 9:9. Then read the Synoptic accounts of the story (Matthew 21:1-11; Mark 11:1-10; Luke 19:28-40) and compare them with the one John describes. What do you think are the major differences between John's account and the other Gospels' accounts of this story? What is John's purpose in placing the episode of the triumphant entry (12:12-18) so closely after Mary's anointing of Jesus?

DAY FIVE: John 12:20-50

What meaning is there in the Greeks' coming to Jesus? Compare 12:27-36 with the accounts of Jesus in the garden of Gethsemane in Matthew 26:36-46; Mark 14:33-36; and Luke 22:40-46. (See also John 18:1.) Read Isaiah 53:1 and 6:10 and compare their Old Testament context with the context in which John uses them in 12:38-41.

DAY SIX:

Read the commentary in the participant book.

LATE AGAIN!

John 10:40-42 feels almost like an ending to the Gospel (and some have proposed that the first draft of John did conclude at this point). Beginning with 11:1, however, the scene shifts to the Bethany that is near Jerusalem (not the one across the Jordan River). The first four verses of the chapter provide a hasty introduction pointing us ahead of the narrative; but it leaves us asking, "Why does Jesus delay his trip to Bethany for two days, especially since he dearly loves this family?"

The disciples are comfortable right where they are and don't want Jesus to go back into hostile territory. Jesus responds that there is a limited time in which to act—we have just so many hours of sunlight before it gets dark (see Jeremiah 13:16). Again, it sounds like Jesus asserts control over his own life. Not even the death of a friend is going to force him to act until he is ready!

In the next verses, Jesus uses sleep as a metaphor for death, but the disciples don't get it. So Jesus must explicitly declare that Lazarus is dead, but he will build their faith in him by what he is about to do. Thomas's statement in 11:16 is strangely pessimistic yet a strong declaration of faith. Going across the river into Judea was like going into enemy territory.

BETTER LATE THAN NEVER

When Jesus arrives, Lazarus has already been in the tomb for four days. Jews in Jesus' day believed a human's "life-breath" (or "spirit") hovered around the tomb for three days before departing. Lazarus was without doubt dead! Notice that *Jewish* friends had gathered to mourn Lazarus and support Mary and Martha. The Bethany family's close relationship with Jesus did not alienate them from the other Jews of their village.

Martha rushes out to meet Jesus and declares (accusingly?) that her brother would not have died had not Jesus tarried about before setting out for Bethany. Her statement is ambiguous. On the one hand, it is an expression of her faith in her friend Jesus, but on the other hand, there may be a hint of anger in her words. The conversation that ensues (11:23-27) is fascinating. Jesus says Lazarus will live again. Martha says yes, he will be resurrected on "the last day." (In the first century, some Jews followed the Pharisees in believing in a resurrection of the dead, while others agreed with the Sadducees, who would not concede that the Torah taught such an idea.) Jesus responds by declaring that he is the "resurrection and the life." Where he is, the last day has already come. Martha affirms her faith in Jesus without really saying that she believes Jesus can raise Lazarus.

Jesus' words in 11:25 are confusing: "I am the resurrection and the life. Those who believe in me, even though they die, will live, and everyone who lives and believes in me will never die." In the second line, it sounds as if believers do die, while the third line seems to say they never die. Perhaps we should take the second line to mean death is a certainty, but life may come from death. Or maybe we could insert the word *really* before "die" in the last line.

In 11:28-32, Mary comes out to meet Jesus and has a conversation similar to Martha's. However, a group of mourners (called "the Jews") accompany her, and the sight of their weeping shocks Jesus. "He was greatly disturbed in spirit and deeply moved" (11:33). In Greek, the statement implies not so much a deep sadness as a profound anger. The word translated as "greatly disturbed" is *embrimaomai* (EM-BRI-MA-O-MAY), and it is used again in 11:38. One scholar has translated the word as "snorted"! But why does the mourning of the crowd evoke Jesus' anger at what death does to humans? His deep emotions are further expressed in another Greek word, *tarassō* (TA-RA-SO), translated in the NRSV as "deeply moved." It means to "shudder" or "shake," expressing deep disturbance. Jesus himself begins to weep. Perhaps what John intends is for us to see Jesus even more moved and troubled at the power of death than we are and then, in that context, revealed to be an even greater power.

When Jesus calls for the stone to be rolled away from the tomb, he was looking at either a hole cut into the side of a mountain or dug deep down on flat land. In each case, the hole was covered with a stone to discourage grave robbers, of whom there were many in Jesus' time. Martha warns him that after four days, the body has begun to decay, but Jesus responds by reminding her that she is about to see a marvelous expression of God's glory. Jesus' prayer is for the sake of the crowd and not his own. Then, with a shout, he commands Lazarus to come out of the tomb, and here Lazarus comes, struggling to move with all of the cloths wrapped around him. Now Jesus calls on the crowd, "Unbind him, and let him go." Christ does the miracle, but then he invites humans to assist him in giving new life. He asks all disciples to participate in the freeing of those he has raised to new life. Can we trust our eyes not to deceive us?

AN UNEXPECTED SIDE EFFECT

We are accustomed to the possibility that the best of medications might have some unpleasant—even deadly—side effects. So, John's narrative moves in 11:45-57 to some serious side effects of Jesus' raising of Lazarus. Oddly enough, in John this wondrous restoration of life sparks the plot to kill Jesus. Some of those present for the raising of Lazarus run to the religious authorities with the news. Quite literally, they can't believe their eyes.

"The council" mentioned in 11:47 (comprised of the chief priests and the Pharisees) refers to the Sanhedrin, the most powerful religious body in the Judaism of Jesus' day (see also 7:32). The statement that Caiaphas was high priest "that year" confuses us. The high priest was an inherited office for a life-time (see Numbers 25:10-13). Possibly the Romans had taken over the appointment of this figure and changed it as often as they wished. Others suggest that the expression *that year* means "that year that changed everything."

The logic of the council's discussion seems odd: If Jesus keeps performing signs, everyone will believe in him; then Rome will get wind of it and come destroy them. Of course, the irony of their argument is that once they killed Jesus, the Romans still came and destroyed them a few years later in the Jewish revolt (66–70 A.D.). Caiaphas adds to the irony by saying more than he intended to say: "It is better for you to have one man die for the people than to have the whole nation destroyed" (11:50). The high priest was not usually a prophet, so his prophetic utterance is entirely unintended. Ultimately Christ did die for the nation and for the world and united us all.

BOTH SIDES NOW

In the opening verses of John 12, we see opposing responses to Jesus, described side by side in the text. First, we see Mary's anointing of Jesus and his triumphal entry, both of which quickly turn sour. At a dinner gathering, Mary brings costly perfume made from a plant grown in the mountains of India, and in an act of extreme love and gratitude, she unknowingly prepares Jesus for his death and burial. However, Judas objects to Mary's extravagance and pretends that he would have given the money to the poor. An excited and curious crowd develops to get a glimpse of Jesus and the miracle man Lazarus; but soon the Pharisees are plotting to kill Lazarus. He has become a walking advertisement for Jesus!

Next, John tells of Jesus' entry into Jerusalem. His account is similar to those found in the Synoptic Gospels except that John does not explicitly say Jesus enters Jerusalem. The scene has an element of nationalism about it, with the waving palms recalling the period of the Maccabees and the crowd's cry in 12:13 of "King of Israel." However, in the face of this nationalistic frenzy, Jesus mounts a young donkey (12:14) in keeping with Zechariah 9:9-10, a picture of a victorious king riding humbly on a donkey—a king of peace, not war.

> **Maccabees**
>
> The family that led the Jewish revolt against the Syrians and the Egyptians in the first century before Christ.

Of course, the disciples did not understand what Jesus had done until after his death and resurrection. The crowd is present only because of the marvel Jesus had done in raising Lazarus. The religious leaders are discouraged and declare that "the world has gone after him!" (John 12:19). Their exaggeration was ironically right again.

THE BEGINNING OF THE END

John 12:20-50 is a text that signals the beginning of the end for Jesus. Most translations call those who come to see Jesus in this instance "Greeks" or *Hellēnes* (HEL-LAY-NES), but the word could also mean "Gentiles" (that is, all those who are not Jews). Interestingly, upon hearing that the Greeks have come and wish to see him, in 12:23 Jesus declares, "The hour has come" (which refers to the arrival of the crucial period of his betrayal and crucifixion). The religious leaders have said in despair that the whole world is running to Jesus, and now a large part of that world does come.

To clarify what he believes will transpire in "the hour," Jesus provides an ominous metaphor: A seed must fall into the ground and die before it grows and yields fruit. In a simple reference to a seed, Jesus explains the meaning of his own death. Further, Jesus warns his hearers that if he is to give up his life, those who would follow him must likewise "lose" their lives—and not just lose their lives; they must also hate their lives. This troubling phrase in 12:25 is one of the most difficult sayings in John. It is John's version of a phrase found with slight variations in Matthew 10:39; Mark 8:35; and Luke 17:33. Does Jesus mean we must literally *hate* our lives? The phrase is typical of John's tendency toward exaggeration and probably does not mean "hate" in our sense of the word. But the idea that we must radically value our authentic, spiritual lives over our physical lives is a difficult teaching to accept, even today.

John's version of Jesus' prayer in 12:27-28 does not take place in the garden of Gethsemane as it does in parallel passages in Matthew 26:36-46; Mark 14:32-42; and Luke 22:39-46. However, Jesus does express the trouble in his soul. In using the word translated as "troubled," Jesus echoes the same kind of sorrow he felt standing before Lazarus' grave (11:33). This is as close as John will bring us to sensing what must have been Jesus' torment over what he knew he must do. Notice that in John, though, Jesus' torment is expressed simply as a question, which immediately receives an answer. The heavenly voice in 12:28 assures Jesus that his death will be his glorification. Of course, the crowd is not sure what it was, but Jesus lets them know the voice was for their bene- fit, not his (12:30).

In the next few verses, Jesus' conversation with the crowd (12:31-36) seems to ramble. Essentially Jesus describes his death as a "lifting up" that will drive evil from the world, and then he makes a marvelous promise: When Jesus is glorified through the cross, he will draw "all people" to him. The crowd is stymied, of course, since they know nothing of the Messiah's being killed, and they wonder what Jesus means by speaking of the "Son of Man." Yet when we seek for understanding what God has done for us in Christ, this verse with its mysterious "drawing" image is powerful. And when Jesus claims he is the light that allows us to escape the darkness of the world (12:35-36), we can be sure of John's point: If we follow the light, we become "children of the light"—just as he said in John 1:1-18.

THE WHYS AND WHEREFORES

In truth, according to 12:37, some people did not believe in Jesus. John tries to explain this by recalling Isaiah 6:10, which accounts for unbelief by refer- ring to God's intentional blinding of certain people. This reference places the unbelieving response to Jesus in the context of the experience of the great Old Testament prophets and raises the thorny issue of how and why God would blind some so that they could not believe, even if they wanted to. This issue is clearly part of the experience of the early church, which struggled to make sense of the rejection of the Christian message (see Matthew 13:13-15; Mark 4:12; Luke 8:10; and Romans 11:8). Ultimately, this idea that God blinds some preserves an element of mystery to the act of faith. It is simply a mystery why there is this resistance to faith among some.

The final verses in John 12 (44-50) summarize the public ministry of Jesus and prepare us for his private ministry with his disciples (John 13–17). What Jesus says here contains a number of important themes.

- Jesus has faithfully represented God, the one who sent him.

- As God's special agent (Son), he has provided light in the darkness of the world.

- His task has not been to judge others but to offer the world genuine life. Those who reject him judge themselves.

- Through Jesus, God gives the world "eternal life" (that is, true life, life as it was intended by our Creator).

As John likely intended, we hear this summary—as did Jesus' disciples—and are prepared for Jesus' final instructions.

INVITATION TO DISCIPLESHIP

Often Christian discipleship develops out of a careful process of assessing whether or not we can believe our eyes, so to speak. While there are aspects of the Christian message we cannot deny, there are likely other aspects that trouble us. Can we truly believe all that Jesus claims to be? Can we accept all that Jesus declares we are to be as his disciples? Can we trust Jesus to provide the light in our dark world? Must we be willing to hate our own lives in order to follow his way of living? Can we put our faith in this Jesus whom so many people completely reject?

The struggle to believe or not to believe our eyes continues—at least in this life. So discipleship always involves an element of trust. Like Martha, we talk like we know what Jesus says about himself is true. Still, he asks us the question "Do you believe this?" and waits for our response.

FOR REFLECTION

- Jesus experiences the terrible pain of seeing a beloved friend die and shares his own tears with others gathered at Lazarus' tomb. Yet this is the one who says he is the resurrection and the life. Confronted with death, we see his genuine humanity. How does that make you feel about your own painful times?

- Commentators differ over the meaning of John 11:25-26. Take time to read the marginal notes on those verses in your study Bible, or look up what has been said about those verses in a Bible commentary. How do you understand what Jesus means?

- John 12:27 and the verses that follow describe how troubled Jesus is about his impending crucifixion. How would you reconcile passages that highlight Jesus' divinity with those that highlight his humanity?

FOR FURTHER REFLECTION

Jesus stood amid the mourners, deeply moved and profoundly angered by the death of his friend Lazarus. Others wept, and so did he. Jesus' encounter with the death of a friend forces us to ask about our relationships with those who are dead or dying. Disciples might profit from hearing once again this sensitive passage from a Meditation by John Donne, a sixteenth-century poet and Anglican priest. Imagine him in his apartment as he hears the church bells tolling for the death of one of the villagers.

> No man is an island, entire of itself; every man is a piece of the continent, a part of the main. If a clod be washed away by the sea, Europe is the less.... Any man's death diminishes me because I am involved in mankind, and therefore never send to know for whom the bell tolls; it tolls for thee. (From *The Norton Anthology of English Literature*, edited by M. H. Abrams [W. W. Norton & Company, Inc., 1979] pages 1108–09.)

How does this understanding of death affect your discipleship?

Would You Believe It?

So if I, your Lord and Teacher, have washed your feet,
you also ought to wash one another's feet.

—John 13:14

INTRODUCTION

One year while I was still teaching, Archbishop Desmond Tutu of South Africa was a visiting professor at my school and actually occupied the office next to mine. With extraordinary warmth, Bishop Tutu came into my office on many occasions to ask how I was doing and to visit with me. We became personal friends. What a gift! Here I was, a small-town boy from Idaho, friends with Desmond Tutu, a winner of the Nobel Prize for Peace. I felt like I was living a dream. I still delight in asking my friends, "Would you believe it? Bishop Tutu and I were friends!" Jesus seemed always to be leading people to ask that same question of themselves and to others: Would you believe it?

DAILY ASSIGNMENTS

DAY ONE: John 13:1-20

What about the story of Jesus' washing the feet of the disciples most impresses you? How do you understand Peter's resistance to Jesus' offer to wash his feet and Jesus' response (13:6-10). Note that in 13:18 we again see Jesus choosing the disciples. How do you interpret what Jesus is doing here? Read Psalm 41; reflect on verse 9 and how it illuminates John 13:18. What questions do you have about this whole story?

DAY TWO: John 13:21-38

Compare John's account of Jesus' last supper to the accounts in Matthew 26:17-30; Mark 14:12-31; and Luke 22:7-38. How does John's account differ from the Synoptic Gospels' accounts? What conclusions do you draw from this comparison? Compare the commandment Jesus gives in 13:34 with what he says in Matthew 5:43-48 and Mark 12:28-34 and with Leviticus 19:18. Why do you think John's version in 13:31-35 focuses on love for "one another" rather than love for God or love for neighbor?

DAY THREE: John 14:1-14

How do you understand the promise of the "many dwelling places" in "my Father's house"? Read Psalms 1:6; 27:11; and 119:26-37 and summarize the meaning of "way" in these passages. How does that help explain John 14:6?

Notice that 14:8-11 addresses again the theme of seeing. What questions do these verses call to mind? What do you think are the "greater works" (8:12) that Jesus says believers will do?

DAY FOUR: John 14:15-24

Compare what these verses tell us about the Advocate and what we learn in later statements in 14:25-26; 15:26; and 16:7. Put these verses in your own words. What is the meaning of *home* in 14:23?

DAY FIVE: John 14:25-31

What do you make of the last part of 14:28: "I am going to the Father, because the Father is greater than I"? Why does John use the expression *the ruler of this world* (14:30) to identify that figure elsewhere known as Satan or the devil? Review John 13–14 to determine what holds Jesus' discourse together.

DAY SIX:

Read the commentary in the participant book.

DIRTY FEET

In John 13, Jesus and the disciples are sharing their last meal together, and Judas has departed to arrange his betrayal of his master. At this point, the Synoptic Gospels narrate what takes place around the table with the meal (Matthew 26:17-30; Mark 14:22-26; Luke 22:15-20); this will provide the basis for the later institution of the Lord's Supper. However, John's account casts its light on something else: the dirty feet of Jesus' disciples. In fact, for John, the meal itself almost seems secondary to what Jesus does with the towel and the water basin.

Although they are easily combined, John offers two interpretations of Jesus' washing the disciples' feet. The first emerges in the discussion between Jesus and Peter in 13:3-11. Jesus seems to say that participating in the foot washing is the acceptance of his death as the means of salvation. In some sense, then, John would have us see the foot washing as a symbol of Jesus' crucifixion. The second interpretation is found in Jesus' words in 13:12-20. Jesus' act is an example of the way the disciples should treat one another. As Jesus served them, so they should serve one another. The servant is in no sense greater than the master of the house, and Jesus is not greater than God. As a result, the meal becomes an occasion for a lesson on servanthood instead of a model for a future sacrament (13:16-18).

Jesus' cryptic words in 13:18-20 echo what he said earlier in 6:64-71. Jesus quotes Psalm 41:9, which speaks of a trusted friend who "lifted the heel against me." Scholars believe that in the Near East, during the time of Jesus, one showed disdain and disrespect for another by showing him or her the bottom of the foot. The point of this incident is to confirm that the disciples know Jesus as the great "I am." The discussion ends with the assertions that any reaction to Jesus constitutes one's reaction to God. Receiving Jesus is the same as receiving God. The radical implication is that we can receive God by allowing God to serve us.

SO CLOSE AND YET SO FAR

The Gospels all include the fact that Judas betrayed Jesus. John emphasizes the tragedy that one who is so close to Jesus cooperates in the plan to execute him. Of course, John suggests that Jesus knew all along what Judas was going to do. Peter goes through the "beloved disciple" to ask Jesus who the betrayer is. The scene (which is the first mention of this anonymous disciple) suggests the fondness Jesus had for this particular disciple and the disciple's fondness for Jesus. All of this accelerates our curiosity. Even Peter has to go through the beloved disciple to ask a question.

Judas is the "son of Simon Iscariot" (13:26), which has aroused lots of curiosity about Simon Iscariot himself. The Greek manuscripts are not clear as to whether it is Simon or Judas himself who is from Iscariot. John is the only Gospel to name Judas' father as Simon Iscariot, so some have doubted the usefulness of this reference. Iscariot refers to "Kerioth," a village in Judah.

Once Judas accepts the piece of bread from Jesus, John tells us that "Satan" entered him. This is the only use of the word *Satan* in John. When Jesus tells Judas to go and do what he must, the others think he is instructing Judas on the purchase of supplies. Judas leaves, and John tells us "it was night." As is often the case, night is not simply a reference to a time period but rather a symbol. Night represents the darkness of evil and opposition. The power of the scene results from the fact that Jesus has just washed Judas' feet, and now Judas leaves to arrange his master's arrest. One so close to Jesus appears to be so far from him. The light and the darkness stand in stark opposition.

STILL SO CLOSE AND YET SO FAR

If you read John 13:31-32 too quickly, you are liable to get dizzy. To oversimplify a much debated verse, the point seems to be that God's presence is revealed in Jesus, and thereby the revelation of God's own self is clarified. The visible expression of God's presence (that is, glory) is found foremost in the cross. In speaking this way, Jesus prepares his disciples for his departure. Notice too that Jesus gives his disciples only one commandment: "Love one another" (13:34). The disciples' love for each other is modeled after the love Jesus has demonstrated (and will demonstrate) for them. This mutual love is the sign of our discipleship for others to see. However, the commandment Jesus declares here is problematic; for in contrast to John, the other Gospels unanimously echo Leviticus 19:18, 34 and report that Jesus' commandment was to love God and neighbor (Matthew 22:34-46; Mark 12:28-34; Luke 10:25-37).

Sadly, a chapter boasting such a radical example of servanthood and such a bold commandment ends with bitter irony: Peter brashly volunteers to lose his life for Jesus. Jesus knows better. Although Peter will indeed lose his life for Christ, Peter will deny that he even knows Jesus before the new day begins. So close and yet so far.

A PLACE FOR US

John 14 begins on a much more joyful note after the prediction of Peter's denial in Chapter 13. Jesus is about to leave the disciples, and he wants them to be clear about two crucial relationships. One is among believers and God *with Christ after death*; the other is between believers and God *in this world before death*.

To make his point, Jesus uses an image of "my Father's house" containing many "dwelling places." The Greek word translated as "dwelling places" is *monai* (MO-NAY), a noun related to the verb *menein* (MA-NAYN), which means to "abide," "dwell," or "remain." (The same verb is used later in 15:4.) *Monai* is sometimes used for a resting place—an inn or motel—along the way where a traveler can stop to get food and rest. The promise is that there is a "place" in God within which they (and by extension, we) can remain. However, the promise applies to the present life as well as the next.

Jesus' announcement that he will "come again" (14:3) and unite believers with him is one of several places (14:18, 28) where Jesus seems to speak of another "coming." However, unlike Mark and Luke, John does not use the word *parousia* (PAR-OU-SEE-AH), which became associated with Jesus' coming again in glory to gather believers (for example, Matthew 24:3 and 1 Thessalonians 2:19). It remains unclear whether this promised coming in John refers to: (1) the time after death when believers are united with Christ; (2) some second coming of Christ into the world; or (3) Christ's presence in the Holy Spirit.

ON THE WAY

The Old Testament term usually translated as "way" often refers to the path a person follows in life (for instance, Psalms 1:6; 27:11; 119:26-37). When Thomas is honest enough to admit that neither he nor his friends know the "way," Jesus declares that he is not only the way but also "the truth, and the life" (14:6). In John's language, all three of these words mean the true, authentic, and meaningful life that God makes available to us through Christ.

What becomes troublesome for many readers is what Jesus says in the second half of 14:6: "No one comes to the Father except through me." Several points are important in reading this verse. First, Jesus is speaking of the other religious options *of his time*. As a result, it is inappropriate to use this verse to reject outright the validity of all other historical religious traditions (many of which are much older than Christianity). The second point is that this voices John's radical exclusiveness most likely reflecting the particular situation of those first Christians to whom John is writing.

Now it is Philip's turn to query Jesus. He asks Jesus to show him the Father (14:8). He obviously has not "caught on" up to this point, but Jesus is patient and makes it clear that seeing him is seeing God. If he cannot believe Jesus' words about this matter, then he can take Jesus' "works" as those of God. These include what God does in Jesus' crucifixion and resurrection. But Jesus goes even further and says, "The one who believes in me will also do the works I do"—and startlingly—"will do greater works" (14:12). But how can that be? We are going to do greater works than those Jesus did? Yes. And notice why: "Because I am going to the Father," Jesus says. How that fact resolves our shock may not be obvious, but it is understandable from John's perspective. When Jesus returns to God, he will empower his followers to do more than he could do as God's agent, limited as he was in time and space. God's work is multiplied by the number of disciples there will be. As remarkable as it may sound, discipleship entails doing greater works than Christ by virtue of being in relationship and in partnership with one another and with God.

WHO IS OUR ADVOCATE?

According to John's Jesus, it is out of love that we keep his commandments. However, that does not mean obeying a lot of rules. While Jesus does speak of commandments in the plural, he issues only one commandment (13:34). Therefore, his notion of "commandments" must refer to the whole way of life toward which Jesus calls us and leads us.

Jesus continues to comfort and confirm his followers by next explaining the role of God's Holy Spirit. John's Gospel offers a new understanding of the Holy Spirit by using an unusual word, *parakletos* (PA-RA-KLAY-TOS). It has been translated as "Comforter" in the King James Version, "Counselor" in the RSV, and "Advocate" in the NRSV. In Greek, the word means something like "one called to your side." It has roots in both the legal and religious spheres of first-century life. As a legal term, a paraclete was a "defense attorney." As a religious term, a paraclete was the content of a promise of consolation. The combination of the two meanings makes the most sense when interpreting its use in John. In 14:16, this figure is called "another Advocate," which suggests that Jesus is the first of the two. The Advocate lives within the believer, even though the world (in the negative sense) cannot receive it.

Ultimately, Jesus assures his disciples that they are not left without guidance when he leaves. The "world" cannot "see" Jesus because it is content within itself. Jesus remains present with his followers through a close-knit fabric of relationships among Father, Son, and Holy Spirit:

Christ is with God. Believers are with Christ. Christ is with us.

This nexus of relationships is key to understanding John's Gospel, and we will return to that later.

Suddenly, another Judas asks a question in 14:22, even though before this, we have heard nothing about him (see Luke 6:16 and Acts 1:13). He asks why Jesus does not reveal himself to the world, and Jesus responds by saying it depends on who loves him. This is essentially the same message we find earlier in 14:1-3. Following this brief exchange, Jesus speaks a second time of the Paraclete in 14:25-26, this time, explicitly calling the Advocate "the Holy Spirit." He describes the Spirit's teaching role and how the Spirit assists us in remembering Jesus. John clearly wants his readers to understand the Paraclete as the way in which God's revelation through Christ is preserved and continued long after Jesus' physical departure.

World

John uses "world" (*kosmos*, KOS-MOS) most often in a negative sense to name the realm of unbelief, the atmosphere in which humans pretend to live out of their own strength. Occasionally, however, it appears John uses the word to name God's creation (see 1:9-10).

Why is the assurance of Christ's presence through the Paraclete such an important point to make? Because the payoff of that assurance is peace. This peace of Christ is not just any peace. It is a peace unlike any the world can give. When the world promises peace, it means a time without the troubles and toil of daily life. And though the world may promise this kind of peace, the world cannot truly deliver it. Peace in John's sense is a life-renewing relationship with Christ. It is not trouble-free. As a matter of fact, it often leads to trouble: the trouble of standing up for justice, loving the unlovable, and dealing with the pains of the world. Nonetheless, Jesus suggests that kind of peace frees us from fear and despair. As one might say goodbye by wishing peace to another person, so Jesus tells his disciples farewell. Yet he doesn't just say goodbye; he promises something of himself will remain with them even though he has gone to the Father. That something is his peace.

John ends this section with Jesus' announcement that the "ruler of this world is coming" (14:30), but that ruler has no power over Jesus. Since for John "world" means the realm of unbelief and separation from God, we should not be surprised to hear Satan spoken of as the prince of that realm of evil.

INVITATION TO DISCIPLESHIP

Our readings in John this week are filled with the failure of the disciples, the very ones on whom Jesus depends for spreading the good news. Judas is the clearest example. But others misunderstand Jesus or ask questions that betray the superficiality of their belief. Peter resists having his feet washed. Thomas has no idea what Jesus is talking about. Philip wants Jesus to show them the Father when seeing Jesus is the same as seeing the Father.

As disciples of Jesus, we would do well to remember how limited our knowledge is and avoid pretending that we know it all. Unfortunately, we often have no occasion in our church communities when we can admit what we don't know. Let us listen for an invitation from Jesus to a discipleship of honesty. Let us look to Jesus for an offer to find and create safe places in our congregations to talk about what matters most in our lives.

FOR REFLECTION

- There is no account of Jesus' institution of the Lord's Supper in John. However, John 13:14 reports that after having washed his disciples' feet, Jesus says, "So if I, your Lord and Teacher, have washed your feet, you also ought to wash one another's feet." When have you experienced foot washing as an occasion of worship?

- Some think the limitation of our love to those who are also disciples (John 13:34-35) reflects the situation of the Christians at the time John wrote. They needed a strong sense of group solidarity over against the opponents who threatened them. How do you understand what Jesus means in 13:34-35?

- What are the implications of Jesus' words "No one comes to the Father except through me" (14:6) for our relationships with other world religions?

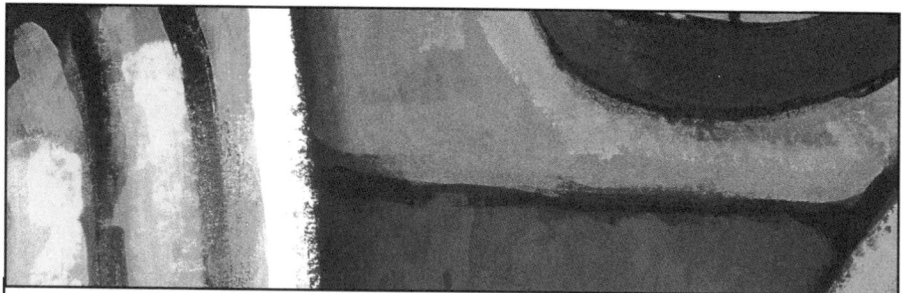

FOR FURTHER REFLECTION

An ancient manuscript purporting to be the Gospel of Judas has been discovered and is now being studied by scholars. It will be years before we can speak definitively of its origin and contents. This codex (an ancient "book" with papyrus sheets) is written in Coptic and was found near Nag Hammadi in eastern Egypt. This site was the source of a number of other ancient documents, including the Gospel of Thomas. Some scholars believe the Gospel of Judas was written sometime between 220 and 340 A.D. and shows signs of having been translated into Coptic from Greek. The current proposal is that it was another of the documents used by Christian groups independent of the "orthodox church."

What is striking about this newly discovered manuscript is that it reports Judas Iscariot did not betray Jesus but rather heroically aided in his plot to be recognized as the Messiah. Jesus asks him to pass on information about Jesus' whereabouts so that Jesus would be arrested. Hence, his plans were fulfilled only with Judas's help. The earliest church rejected this view of Judas and developed the one we find in our Gospels.

What do you think of these understandings of Judas? What value would more historical information about Judas have in your understanding of the Jesus story?

What Time Is It?

I have said these things to you in figures of speech.
The hour is coming when I will no longer speak to you in figures,
but will tell you plainly of the Father.

—John 16:25

INTRODUCTION

With the schedule many of us have, knowing what time it is becomes a necessity. We must know what time to be at work, what time to arrive at the rehearsal, what time to pick up the kids at school, what time to have the evening meal ready, what time the game starts, what time to meet a friend for coffee, what time to feed the pets, and so on. Some say we are addicted to time, and they refuse to wear a watch. Yet whether we carry with us a timepiece or not, we cannot escape from the fact that time is important; and the older we get, the more likely we are to acknowledge just how important it is.

As the revelation of God, Jesus actually spent significant time on earth in the presence of his disciples. The story of Jesus in John makes it clear just how crucial time was, for the climax of his ministry came when his "hour" arrived.

DAILY ASSIGNMENTS

DAY ONE: John 15:1-17

Pay attention to those verses that include the word *abide*. What do you think is the central point of the image of the vine? Read these Old Testament passages and consider how each helps us understand today's passage from John: Psalm 80:8-16; Isaiah 5:1-7; 27:2-6; Jeremiah 2:21; Ezekiel 15:1-6; 17:5-10; 19:10-14. Now read Matthew 21:33-46; Mark 12:1-12; and Luke 20:9-19, and consider which of those passages is most helpful in interpreting John 15:1-8. How is the image of the vine and branches related to what follows in 15:9-17?

DAY TWO: John 15:18–16:4a

Note how often the word *hate* is used in these verses. Why do you think Jesus uses such a drastic term, and what do you think he means? What does 15:26-27 add to your knowledge of the Paraclete? In 16:1-4, Jesus sounds as if he is preparing his disciples for a period of persecution. How would such preparation help them?

DAY THREE: John 16:4b-15

What does this passage add to your understanding of the Paraclete? Summarize what you know about the Paraclete from all these passages together:

14:15-17, 25-26; 15:26-27; 16:7-15. What do you think is John's purpose in using the word *Paraclete* rather than *Spirit* or *Holy Spirit*?

DAY FOUR: John 16:16-24

What does the expression *a little while* mean, and why does Jesus use it? What meaning is conveyed by the metaphor of a woman in childbirth (16:20-22)? What does Jesus mean by saying, "Until now you have not asked for anything in my name" (16:24)?

DAY FIVE: John 16:25-33

Why does Jesus say he has spoken to the disciples in figures of speech yet will no longer do so during "the hour that is coming"? How is Jesus a mediator between God and us? How does Jesus' impending crucifixion fulfill what he says will happen in 16:31-33? What does Jesus mean when he says he has conquered the world?

DAY SIX:

Read the commentary in the participant book.

A PLACE TO ABIDE

Anyone who has ever pulled vines out of a garden knows that they are quite messy. So at first, it may seem strange to readers today that Jesus uses the vine and its tangle of branches as a metaphor for the Christian's relationship with him and God. Of course, if we were all grape growers and wine makers, it would be a different matter. Or we could simply recall our study of the Old Testament: The vineyard is an ancient image for Israel and its relation with God. For John's audience, the use of the vine as a metaphor would not have seemed strange at all.

Abide

This translates the Greek verb *menō* (MEN-O) and refers to a close relationship, such as "Abide in me as I abide in you" (John 15:4).

John 15 uses the vine as an allegory to suggest the complex relationship among Jesus, God, and the believer. According to Jesus' speech, God is the vine-grower, Jesus is the vine, and believers are the branches. When he refers to pruning in 15:2, Jesus likely means clearing away rather than cutting off (the Greek adjective is *katharoi* [KATH-AH-ROY] and most often means "cleaning"). By believing Jesus' word, the disciples have been cleansed. Then Jesus speaks of the branches' "fruit" as the disciples' acts of love. However, only in a relationship with Jesus (15:4) can the disciples bear fruit—that is, love. Of course, the key word in all that Jesus says here is *abide*. Recall that this same word appeared earlier in John 1:38 and referred to the place Jesus was staying. Here it may be understood simply as "relate."

Jesus' warning in 15:6 sounds very much like judgment, but we should not import our contemporary imaginings of a fiery hell into John. More than likely Jesus intended to communicate the idea that outside of a relationship with him, life becomes empty and meaningless, much as fruitless vines are barren and worthless. Acts of love identify a disciple and illumine God's presence. Disciples in close relationship with Christ will absorb and be nourished by his teachings, thus assuring that prayers are answered (15:7). This verse echoes the promise that God answers prayers offered in Jesus' name (14:13-14). Jesus shifts the emphasis slightly in 15:9 so that living in relationship with Christ is equated with living in love. The next verse, 15:10, sounds a bit strange because Jesus has given the disciples only one commandment, and that is to love one another. However, in John, Jesus uses the plural "commandments," suggesting that loving involves all of one's acts and being—indeed, one's whole life. The complete "joy" Jesus promises in 15:11 is like the "peace" he promised earlier in 14:27, in that it arises from the relationship of intimacy with Jesus.

YOU'VE GOT A FRIEND

In 15:12, Jesus repeats the commandment to love but enriches it by describing it as the same love Christ has for us. Of course, Jesus loves by dying for us, so loving as he loves us means our willingness to sacrifice our lives for others. Love is a mighty power that calls for the most radical of sacrifices.

Jesus continues to make such stunning pronouncements. In 15:13-17, elaborating on what he means by loving others, Jesus calls his disciples "friends." The Greek word translated as "friends" is *philoi* (PHIL-LOI), a term that comes from one of the three Greek verbs that mean "to love." This is friendship love. The disciples are not servants but friends, because they know what Jesus is doing. As common and acceptable as this idea of friendship love may seem to us today, the implications were profound and no doubt startling for John's first hearers. Think of being Jesus'/God's friend!

In contrast to all this talk of love, Jesus reminds his followers that the world hates Jesus and his followers precisely because Jesus calls them out of the world. (Remember, *world* in John often means the realm of evil.) Since Jesus is not "of the world," neither are his disciples. The servants cannot expect to be treated well if the master is not (15:18-20).

The bold claim of 15:24-25 is that the revelation of God through Christ makes sin clear. In other words, those who reject the revelation have no way of discerning what sin is; but neither do they have any excuse for sinning. In an odd sort of way, Jesus *causes* sin by leaving those who reject him without any excuse for sinning.

SIDE BY SIDE

The disciples' plight in the world is changed by the presence of the Paraclete (15:26-27). By our side in this struggle in the world, the Paraclete whispers in our ears (that is, "testifies to") the truth of God's presence in Christ. (Note that in 15:26 Jesus himself sends the Paraclete, while in 14:16

God sends the Paraclete.) Because of the witness of the Paraclete, disciples are also witnesses.

In John 16, Jesus shifts the subject of his speech back to his departure. This announcement has already caused his disciples sorrow (14:1). Now, in 16:2, Jesus again uses the expression *put out of the synagogue* in anticipating what they can expect. Those who are guilty of expelling the disciples from the synagogue will have their "hour." This is one of the few times the word *hour* is used for those who oppose Jesus. Here, it means the "decisive time," or the time when Jesus' opponents will experience the consequences of their actions.

As painful as it may be, by his leaving, Jesus is able to send the Advocate (Paraclete) to the disciples. Christ and the Paraclete work in tandem so that the Paraclete's work fills the gap left when Jesus goes away. In what may be the most difficult of the Paraclete passages, in 16:7-15 Jesus describes the role of the Paraclete in terms of finding the world guilty regarding sin, righteousness, and judgment. We might paraphrase Jesus' clarification this way: The world is guilty of sin because it rejects Jesus as the Christ; the world is guilty of unrighteousness because it rejects Christ's death (and departure) as God's victory; and the world is guilty of judgment because it rejects the truth that in Christ, evil has already been condemned and defeated.

Essentially, the Paraclete's role is to prove the world wrong and Christ's followers right. The Advocate—this one who is promised to be by our side—affirms the truthfulness of our belief in Jesus and assures us of the fundamental value of our witness of Jesus as the Christ.

In 16:12-15, Jesus continues his discussion of the Paraclete, making clear that he will leave this world in a short time, but in an equally short time, the disciples will see him again. What he means is that in his crucifixion, he will be absent for a time, but in the gift of the Paraclete he will once again be present. So only after Jesus' resurrection and the gift of the Spirit will the disciples be led to the full truth. The role of the Paraclete is to communicate the whole revelation in Christ. "What is mine" means the content of the message and mission God gives Christ. The one by our side makes Christ present again.

A LITTLE WHILE

Jesus goes on in 16:16-24 to address a puzzling topic he took up earlier in the chapter: what he means by "a little while" (16:18). The expression seems to mean a decisive moment, a vital time when God acts. Jesus explains his words by saying that the disciples' feelings will be reversed, that they will, in a way, turn an emotional somersault. By way of illustration, Jesus compares the coming pain of his leaving with the pain of childbirth and the joy of birthing a new being—pain turned to joy (16:21). When the disciples see Jesus again, they will rejoice, and their pain will be a thing of the past. In the meantime, though, according to the last part of 16:23, "if you ask anything of the Father in my name, he will give it to you." In other words, the Paraclete will enable them to want what God desires them to want. The Paraclete will cleanse their prayers of selfish motives so that their "joy may be complete" (16:24).

I CAN SEE CLEARLY NOW

Jesus' speech so far in these passages has sometimes sounded like riddles, but here in 16:25-33, he promises a time when he will speak without metaphors and when the disciples will understand (if they ask in his spirit). By implication, the Paraclete continues to clarify Jesus' teachings for our day. According to what Jesus says in 16:26-27, believers can ask God directly without going through Jesus, thanks to the revelation of God's love in Christ.

However, in 16:29-32, Jesus tempers the disciples' confidence. A time ("the hour") is coming when they will abandon Jesus and scatter. (He is surely speaking here of his arrest and crucifixion.) Still, Jesus is never alone because God is always with him. All of this discussion comes down to one point: The disciples will see Jesus' teachings clearly and therefore have peace. They will be persecuted, but they can take courage because Christ has "conquered the world" (16:33), so they can live in that promise of peace. Obviously peace in persecution is a kind of peace different from what the world offers; nonetheless, Jesus bestows upon them the promise of his kind of peace.

FAREWELL FOR NOW

The so-called "Farewell Discourses" in John 13:31–16:33 constitute the last occasion on which Jesus taught his disciples in private. By Jesus' time, the farewell speech was a common literary form, the best example of which is found in Deuteronomy 31 and 32, where Moses provides for the future leadership of the people of Israel. So, John follows a standard form in Chapters 13–16. Jesus prepares the disciples for his leaving and assures them of the continuing presence of the Paraclete. It is the kind of thing a pastor might do in her or his final sermon to a congregation. Jesus speaks of the fear of the loss of God's presence. It is a fear many of us have from time to time. However, Jesus' promise of the Paraclete assures us that God is always present.

Farewell Discourses

The lengthy speeches of Jesus recorded in John 13:31–16:33 are often called the "Farewell Discourses," because in this Gospel, these are Jesus' final teachings before his crucifixion. Anyone looking for some structure or pattern will likely find these chapters difficult. They seem broken into smaller pieces, but even then they do not demonstrate any logical development. Many have proposed that they are a compilation of originally separate and smaller pieces. However, others have argued that the three chapters are a single unity, but not necessarily a logical one.

INVITATION TO DISCIPLESHIP

Sometimes we need to know what time it is. In a sense, it is always a crucial time, a time of decision (*kairos*). We need not expect that Jesus is returning tomorrow. We need not worry that we might be "left behind." But there is not a moment of our lives when we do not have to choose between discipleship and the world. What or who will determine our fundamental beliefs and motives? And even if we don't believe that the "world" is entirely a realm of evil, our experience shows us that at times this world corners us, confronts us, and demands our decision. Very simply, discipleship means choosing God's love and acceptance as our highest priority every minute of every day, no matter what the situation.

F O R   R E F L E C T I O N

John 14:15-17, 25-26; 15:26-27; 16:7-15

- Go through the passages listed above that speak of the Paraclete, and for each one summarize the meaning the Spirit has for your life. Don't just rewrite what the passages say. Make your list personal, private, and even confessional. For instance, you might summarize part of the meaning of 16:7-15 for yourself in this way:

I am constantly comparing myself with others who seem more successful, more intelligent, and most certainly more prosperous. The result is that I feel inferior and a failure. I know I make these judgments on the basis of the values of our North American culture: success, wealth, status, and popularity. However, the Spirit keeps nudging me to recognize how wrong the culture is and calling me back to my basic faith in Christ.

FOR FURTHER REFLECTION

Read Paul's farewell to the elders in Ephesus in Acts 20:17-38 and compare it to Jesus' farewell in John 15–16. What similarities between the two do you see? How are the two speeches different? What would comfort you the most when one of your spiritual leaders or friends in faith is leaving you?

Look Out!

They came there with lanterns and torches and weapons.
Then Jesus, knowing all that was to happen to him, came forward
and asked them, "Whom are you looking for?"
They answered, "Jesus of Nazareth." Jesus replied,
"I am he."...They stepped back and fell to the ground.

—John 18:3-6

INTRODUCTION

I recall an occasion when I wished I had shouted, "Look out!" It was after dark, and a friend and I were walking home from a meeting at the local church. We came to the crosswalk at a busy road. I paused to wait at the curb, but my friend started out to cross the street, planning, I supposed, to go just far enough to shorten our wait for the traffic. Unfortunately, the lights of the oncoming traffic blinded a driver so that he did not see my friend and struck him. My friend suffered a broken hip from which he never entirely recovered. And I still regret that I did not warn him of the danger that was approaching.

Reading the story of Jesus, there comes a point in the plot where readers want to call out to Jesus, "Watch out! It's a trap! The soldiers are coming!" Even if we believe that Jesus knew what faced him, we still wish someone would have warned him. In this week's readings, we have reached that point.

DAILY ASSIGNMENTS

DAY ONE: John 17:1-19

What is the theme of these verses? What does the abundant use of the term *glorify* mean in this passage? What is the subject of Jesus' prayer in 17:1-5, and to what subject does it shift in 17:6-18? How does the later half of 17:11 inform your concept of the unity of the church? What does 17:15 say about the nature of discipleship?

DAY TWO: John 17:20-26

Who or what is the subject of the beginning of this part of Jesus' prayer? This prayer seems to take the place of the Synoptic Gospels' accounts of Jesus' prayer in the garden of Gethsemane. Take time to read those three accounts (Matthew 26:36-46; Mark 14:32-42; Luke 22:40-46) and then compare them to this passage in John.

DAY THREE: John 18:1-14

Read the accounts of Jesus' arrest and trial before the religious leaders in Matthew 26:47-68; Mark 14:43-65; and Luke 22:47-54, 63-71. Note the important differences between John's account and the others. What themes does John uniquely emphasize?

DAY FOUR: John 18:15-27

What is the point of telling the story of Peter's denial of Jesus? What do you think of Jesus' self-defense? Jesus claims he has not taught secretly. Given the content of John 13–16, is that claim true?

DAY FIVE: John 18:28-40

What do you think Pilate is trying to do in the course of his trial of Jesus? What does Jesus mean by saying that his kingdom is not from this world? What do you think Pilate wants to know by asking Jesus, "What is truth" (18:38)?

DAY SIX:

Read the commentary in the participant book.

A FATHER-AND-SON CHAT

John seldom records Jesus' prayers, but John 17 is an exception. It has been called "the high priestly prayer" because, after having spoken at great length to his disciples, Jesus turns his gaze toward God and prays for: (1) his own relationship with God (17:1-5); (2) his disciples (17:6-19); and (3) other believers (17:20-26).

Glorify and Glorification

Designates God's immediate and visible presence. It suggests the awesome quality of the divine in the human world. See Exodus 16:1-10. The divine presence in Jesus is mentioned in John 1:14 and 17:1-5.

The much-anticipated "hour" has finally come, and Jesus asks that God "glorify" him. If glorification is the revelation of God's presence in the world, then Jesus is asking that God manifest God's self through his suffering and death. It is a mutual glorification, because if God's presence shines through Jesus, then both are glorified. The early Christians frequently said that God could be seen in Christ's suffering, but John makes that point indisputable.

In 17:2-4, Jesus speaks of the "authority" God has given him—an authority to bring true life, that is, "eternal life to all whom you [God] have given him" (17:2). *Eternal life* is defined here as knowing God and Christ, so true life is found in a relationship with God the Creator. Jesus says that his death and resurrection will return him to his heavenly glory (a reference back to 1:1-5). So we are not off base, then, to think of the Passion story as the conclusion of Christ's incarnation of God and the beginning of his return to God.

The prayer for the disciples dominates this chapter, using fourteen of its twenty-six verses. Jesus describes his disciples as those God has given him and those who have received God's word through Christ. Hence, disciples know the "truth," meaning the true character of life and its roots in the Creator (17:8). The disciples have knowledge of what God has given Christ, that Jesus comes from God, and that God sent Jesus. Interestingly, believers are represented as knowing God's plan and Christ's message. However, the knowledge is not just some "intellectual comprehension." In this context, *knowing* means full participation, wholeness in a relationship.

Notice that in his prayer, Jesus does not discount the "world." Of course, Jesus does not pray for the world, but he also does not pray that the disciples be taken out of the world. The disciples' place is in the midst of the confusion and distortion of the world. If the Gospel of John sometimes sounds as though Christians should withdraw from the world, Jesus' prayer corrects that misconception. The mission of Jesus—and thus that of his followers—is accomplished *in* the world, not outside it. Because the disciples have received God's message ("word"), the world hates them since they are not "of" (*ek*) the world. They do not draw their purpose for life from the world any more than Jesus did. However, they should continue to be in the world and not be taken out of it (17:16).

John uses the word *sanctify* in 17:17-19, the only place it appears in John. The word is translated from a Greek word, *hagiazō* (HOG-E-A-ZO), which means to "make holy," "set apart," "dedicate," and "purify." It is the same word translated as "hallowed" in the Lord's Prayer in Luke 11:2 and the same word Paul uses in 1 Corinthians 6:11, translated as "sanctified." What Jesus implies is that God's truth makes them holy and protects them while they are in the world. This does not mean some special status, like a super-Christian, pure of sin. It does suggest, though, that faith becomes the center and driving force of a disciple's life.

Thus sanctified, the disciples have been sent into the world. John 17:18 makes the remarkable suggestion that the disciples are sent into the world in the same way God sent Christ into the world (see 20:21). In other words, we have the same mission for God that Jesus had.

The final part of Jesus' prayer widens the circle to include all who may believe as a result of the disciples' ministry (17:20). They too will be made one, purified, and glorified. They are loved by God and Christ. They will make known that God sent Jesus.

The prayer's conclusion is Jesus' commitment to his mission (17:24-26). He will make God's will known throughout the world in order that "the love with which you have loved me may be in them, and I in them." The climax of the prayer, then, is the vision of a message of love that reaches all humans, wherever they may be. That is Jesus' vision for the mission of his disciples.

MOB MENTALITY

The change of tone and subject matter is abrupt at the opening of John 18. After lingering on Jesus' discourses in the previous several chapters, John moves quickly to describe Jesus' arrest. In John, the garden in which Jesus is arrested is in Kidron, the valley just east of Jerusalem. Although this is the first we hear of this place, John tells us Jesus often met there with the disciples (18:2), so Judas knows where to go to find his former master and colleagues. Interestingly, Judas brings a crowd with him. John calls it a "detachment" (18:3), which translates a Greek word for the Latin term *cohort*—technically six hundred soldiers! By the way the word is used here, we can be sure the precise number varied. In any case, picture a relatively large group of Roman soldiers along with some of the Temple police who guard the chief priests and Pharisees, all walking with Judas to find Jesus. It's almost laughable—all these armed men along with the religious officials coming out to subdue and bring in one Galilean prophet! Imagine John smiling. Be sure to note how John describes their coming: They must use lanterns and torches to find their way through the darkness, John's shorthand for evil (18:3). Note too that Jesus already knows what is going to happen to him. None of this comes as a surprise to him (18:4).

When the leaders tell Jesus they are looking for "Jesus of Nazareth," he responds with the powerful words *I am* (not "I am he," as the NRSV has it). The two simple words send soldiers and police tumbling to the ground. Their strength and weapons cannot stand up against the presence of God! A second time Jesus asks whom they are looking for, and they finally start to arrest him. Notice that in John, Judas does not kiss Jesus to betray him into the hands of the soldiers. Jesus is the one who identifies himself to his enemies; he is fully aware his "hour" has come. He even protects his disciples from arrest so that the words of his prayer (17:12) are true and no one is lost.

As in the other Gospels, Peter draws his sword and slices off the ear of one of the slaves. John even tells us the slave's unusual name, which adds realism to the scene (18:10). Yet in John, Jesus is not at all surprised by the impetuous Peter. "Put your sword back into its sheath" (18:11), Jesus says calmly. In the same verse, he speaks of drinking the "cup that the Father has given me." He also speaks of this cup in Matthew 26:39; Mark 14:36; and Luke 22:42. But if in the other Gospels Jesus seems anxious in speaking of the cup of suffering he is about to experience, in John Jesus seems to have it firmly in his grasp.

THE HIGH PRIEST WANTS TO SEE YOU

At this point in John's narrative, there are some confusing statements not easily explained. Jesus is taken to Annas, who we are told "was the father-in-law of Caiaphas, the high priest that year" (18:13). Annas was high priest for a time, but the Romans then apparently stripped him of his position around 15 A.D. John refers to Annas as the high priest several times (18:15, 16, 19, and 22), even though he again explicitly calls Caiaphas the high priest in 18:24. It is likely that people in the first century continued to address those who had previously held the office with the title *high priest*, much as we address former presidents as "Mr. President." That may be the case here.

Imagine John now as a kind of camera operator, moving the camera lens back and forth between Peter and Jesus, deliberately framing the sharp contrasts between Peter's denials and Jesus' faithfulness. The movement goes something like this:

Peter Outside: First accusation and first denial. We see Peter (18:15-18), standing outside the courtyard gate, then allowed in, only to catch the wary eye of a woman who questions him.

Jesus Inside: First defense and first blow. The camera moves to Jesus (18:19-24), who stands before the high priest, is interrogated, then defends himself, saying simply that he has done or said nothing "in secret."

Peter Outside: Second accusation and second denial. The scene shifts back to the courtyard (18:25-27). Along comes someone who was in the garden earlier—a witness against Peter.

Peter Outside: Third accusation and third denial. Then the rooster crows at the rising sun, and the scene begins to fade away. Jesus' prediction proves to be true.

Jesus Outside: Being taken to Pilate (18:28).

The contrast is vivid and dramatic: Human frailty trembles even as Jesus' strength shimmers. We recoil at Peter, not because we are disgusted with him, but because we know ourselves too well. We are Peter.

THE FEDERAL JUDGE

In dealing with Jesus, the religious authorities' hands are tied unless the Roman governor endorses their charges against Jesus and puts him to death. This is why Jesus is taken before Pilate, the ruler of Judea from 26–36 A.D. In Judea, as elsewhere in the empire, the Romans preferred to appoint indigenous leaders to rule their provinces. Pilate governed for ten years without ever understanding the Jewish people. Yet the Jews could execute a criminal only after receiving the official's permission.

Early in the morning, the day before the Passover celebration, the religious leaders bring Jesus to Pilate's headquarters. Because of the threat of defilement during the Passover season, Jews could not enter a Gentile's dwelling (18:28-29). Pilate wonders why he should be involved in this matter, and he is reminded that the Jews cannot impose a death penalty. So, still reluctant to become involved, Pilate goes inside, and Jesus is brought behind him.

Truth

Has to do with the meaning of God's revelation in Christ and its importance for humans. Refers to the most vital truth for us. See John 14:4-7 and 17:17-19.

The discussion between Jesus and Pilate is nothing else if not fascinating (18:33–19:16). John takes his time revealing how Pilate carefully handles this man Jesus. Pilate goes to the heart of the issue right away by asking Jesus, "Are you the King of the Jews?" Jesus is evasive, so Pilate asks more generally, "What have you done?" The discussion turns to the matter of Jesus' kingdom, which Jesus says, as he has before, is "not from [*ek*] this world." Pilate jumps on those words: "So you are a king?" Jesus counters by saying he came into the world to witness to the truth (that is, as the word is used in this Gospel). Pilate responds with sarcasm—we can almost see his lip curling as he asks, "What is truth?" (18:38). Ironically, Pilate is like so many other figures in John's Gospel: He unwittingly asks the right question.

The chapter ends with Pilate's first declaration to the crowd. He cannot convict Jesus of anything and suggests a compromise. To pacify the Jews, it was his practice to release one prisoner at Passover. The crowd cries out for the release not of Jesus but of a robber named Barabbas (whose name ironically means "son of the father [Abba]"). The tension mounts.

INVITATION TO DISCIPLESHIP

A constant encounter with the Passion story is our inescapable call to faith and service. Jesus has said we should love as he loved us—loved us enough to give up his life. However, when discipleship becomes a threat for us (as it did for Peter), we find ourselves in a bind. How much must we give up in the name of discipleship? Are we not entitled to preserve our livelihood as Peter did? Most of us who strive to be Christ's followers will never face the choice between discipleship and death. Is it not, though, a kind of loss, like death, that frightens us from affirming our faith? Is it the loss (or death) of our luxury, our security, our independence, our reputation, our notions of peace and quiet? In surrendering his life out of love for us, Jesus draws us to his cross and confronts us with what we must surrender to be his followers.

FOR REFLECTION

- Some scholars have found what they think are fragments of the Lord's Prayer (Matthew 6:9-13 and Luke 11:2-4) in Jesus' prayer in John 17. Compare the two passages with John 17 and see if you can find similarities among them. How would you approach John 17 differently if you found it contained echoes of the Lord's Prayer?

- Jesus' prayer petitions God for the unity of his disciples. Such petitions seem appropriate today with Christianity's fragmentation into denominations. Do you think the prayer is a legitimate basis and argument for Christian unity?

- John's picture of Peter shows a disciple who demonstrates on the one hand absolute devotion to Jesus (for instance, the footwashing and attacking those who arrest Jesus) and on the other the cowardice of his three denials. What makes Peter tick? How do you related to him?

- To what extent do you think royal (kingship) language is appropriate to use for Jesus? Do our references to Jesus as King betray a misconception of his role in the world and our lives? What words and phrases might we employ to replace the use of the words *king* and *kingdom* to describe the nature of Christ?

FOR FURTHER REFLECTION

John seems quite intentional in placing Peter's denials and Jesus' courage alongside each other in Chapter 18. One commentator proposes that Peter's denials are set in deliberate opposition to Jesus' "I am" declarations during his arrest. Three times John uses Jesus' "I am" to describe his response to his captors (18:5, 6, and 8). Three times John expresses Peter's denials using the same "I am" language, only in the negative. In the first two instances, Peter voices the denials himself: "I am not" (18:17, 25). In the third instance, the "I" comes from the speech of the slave who questions Peter (18:26).

How does this comparison put into perspective your own temptations to deny Christ in word or deed? How does Christ's courage and persistence illumine your own cowardice and instability?

Believing Without Seeing

Jesus said to him [Thomas], "Have you believed because you have seen me? Blessed are those who have not seen and yet have come to believe."

—John 20:29

INTRODUCTION

Seeing something for ourselves is usually important. If we read a review of a particular movie telling us it is the best film of the year, often we will rush to buy our tickets so we can see for ourselves if the claim is true. Then there are times when we may not be able to see a film and must trust the witness of others whom we trust. Similarly, many of us may think that if only we could have seen the risen Christ with our own eyes, we would surely believe. Indeed, the Gospel of John even stresses how faith arises from witnessing Jesus with our own eyes. However, the last appearance of the risen Christ to the disciples reported in John 20 throws us a curve. Can we truly believe without seeing?

DAILY ASSIGNMENTS

DAY ONE: John 19:1-16

Why does Pilate seem to want Jesus released? What are his possible motives? Why is Pilate frightened in the process of sentencing (19:8)? Why does Jesus not defend himself? Why does the crowd say they declare Caesar their king? According to 19:16, who does John say is responsible for the crucifixion?

DAY TWO: John 19:17-42

Compare the account of the crucifixion in John with those in the Synoptic Gospels (Matthew 27:33-66; Mark 15:22-47; Luke 23:33-56). What is the meaning of the words Jesus speaks from the cross to his mother and the beloved disciple? Read Exodus 12:46; Numbers 9:12; and Psalm 34:20. How do they relate to Jesus' crucifixion? What is the meaning in the blood and water that flow from Jesus' side in 19:34?

DAY THREE: John 20:1-18

Why does Peter not "see and believe," whereas the other unnamed disciple does? What do you think about Mary Magdalene at first not being able to recognize the risen Christ? How does Jesus' use of her name in 20:16 enable her to know who is speaking to her?

DAY FOUR: John 20:19-29

What are the important features of this story of Jesus' appearance to the disciples? How do Jesus' words to his disciples in 20:23 define your own mission in the world? Compare John's version of the authorization of the disciples' power to forgive sins with Matthew 16:19 and 18:18. What is the power that Jesus confers on his followers and, by extension, the church? What do you think of Thomas's refusal to believe the disciples when they share their experience of the risen Christ with him? How do you interpret the meaning of 20:29?

DAY FIVE: John 20:30-31

What do these verses tell you, if anything, about the writer of this Gospel and the purpose behind it? Now read how other Gospel writers close their accounts: Matthew 28:16-20; Mark 16:9-20; Luke 24:44-53. What do those verses tell you about the purposes of their Gospels?

DAY SIX:

Read the commentary in the participant book.

JESUS AND PILATE, CONTINUED

The story of Jesus' trial before Pilate continues in John 19, with the Romans' having Jesus beaten and mocked (19:1-2). Of course, their intent is to demoralize their victim as well as punish him to such an extent that the crucifixion would kill him sooner rather than later. Pilate shows him to the crowd, still believing Jesus is innocent. Apparently he still hopes that the crowd will plead for his release. Pilate's cry "Here is the man!" in 19:5, while prompting much speculation, means simply that Pilate is trying to shame Jesus.

Even though he still thinks Jesus is innocent, Pilate invites the crowd to put him to death (19:6). The crowd (called "the chief priests and the police") claims Jesus equates himself with God by calling himself the "Son of God" and, according to the Law, should die. Technically, Leviticus 24:16 does declare blasphemy punishable by death (see John 10:33-38). As a Roman official bound to uphold Roman law, Pilate would have little reason to be intimidated by the crowd's appeal to Jewish law. So the reason for Pilate's fear in 19:8 is not entirely clear, especially since we have not been told previously that he was fearful. If he was concerned that Jesus did claim to be God, Pilate may have thought that Jesus possessed dangerous, magical powers.

Whatever the reason, Pilate retreats into his fortress with the criminal and takes a new approach to his inquisition. "Where are you from?" he asks (19:9). Jesus remains silent. Pilate, seemingly a-bluster with aggravation, then threatens Jesus with his power over life and death. In response, Jesus claims Pilate has no real power, except that which God has given him, and therefore the real sin is that of the captors (19:10-11).

Pilate in History

According to an inscription carved into a limestone block discovered in Caesarea Maritima, Pontius Pilate's official title was "Prefect." He governed the Roman province of Judea from 26 A.D. until he was removed from office in 36 A.D. According to the ancient Jewish historian Josephus, Pilate's authorization of the slaughter of a group of Samaritans in 35 A.D. prompted his recall to Rome.

That wasn't exactly what Pilate wanted to hear. Yet he persists in his efforts to win Jesus' release until the unruly crowd finally attacks his most vulnerable spot in 19:12. Appeals to Caesar by citizens of Rome's empire had been known to result in an official's dismissal. So at this point, Pilate gives up any effort to save Jesus and goes out to the crowd where he sits on the judge's bench (19:13). This "Stone Pavement" or "Gabbatha" may refer to what might have been a paved block on which crucial judgments were made.

Ultimately, Pilate gives in, mocking the crowd by calling Jesus their king. They insist on his crucifixion. In one of the most tragic acts in John, the crowd declares, "We have no king but the emperor" (19:15). The Jewish tradition was a persistent and unyielding refusal to submit to any ruler except God. Now, ironically, the Jews reject their own tradition. John unfortunately ends the story of the trial with the implication that the "them" in 19:16 is the Jews (which of course is not true, as 19:23 shows). Those inclined to do so take this verse as evidence that the Jews killed Jesus.

ATOP THE SKULL

Although John shows a special interest in identifying the fulfillment of Scripture in Jesus' crucifixion, his Gospel shares a good deal in common with the other Gospel accounts. Pilate will not go away! In spite of the Jewish leaders' outrage, he insists on putting the sign on the cross declaring this crucified one "The King of the Jews" (19:19-22). The sign is written in three languages (Hebrew, Greek, and Latin), ironically proclaiming the universal meaning of Jesus' death.

Only women were usually allowed at the foot of a crucified person since the soldiers did not regard them as dangerous. In this case, gathered at the cross were Jesus' mother (never named in John), his mother's sister, "Mary the wife of Clopas, and Mary Magdalene," along with "the disciple whom he loved" (19:25-26). In 19:26-27, Jesus calls the beloved disciple his mother's son, and he calls his mother the mother of this nameless disciple. Why did Jesus say this? There might be a historical reason: With Jesus gone, his mother would have no source of support, and the beloved disciple takes that responsibility. There may also be a theological reason: John 1:12 declares that Jesus would create a new family of God, since believers were given "power to become children of God." In creating a mother-son relationship, the crucified Jesus begins the formation of God's new family.

Jesus has now finished his mission in the world. After asking for water (see John 4:7) and taking some "sour wine," he declares, "It is finished." He then voluntarily "bowed his head and gave up his spirit" (19:28-30). The English translations often supply the pronoun *his* or definite article *the* before the word *spirit*. The Greek sentence has no such pronoun or article and hence might mean "a" spirit. Which spirit, we wonder....

Executioners need to know for sure that their victims are dead. Because a Jewish holiday would soon begin, they hurry this process by thrusting a spear into Jesus' side. As a result of the spear thrust, "blood and water" flow out of Jesus' side (19:34). Some commentators believe this means nothing more than that Jesus is for certain dead. Others propose that John intended for the blood and water to symbolize Holy Communion and baptism.

John again suggests that several Scripture passages were brought to their ultimate meaning by this event, namely Exodus 12:46; Numbers 9:12; and Psalm 34:20. Not only was Jesus crucified on a Friday (the day of preparation for the sabbath) but also the day before the Passover celebration. Hence, Jesus died at the very time the Passover lambs were being slain for the meal the next day. On the other hand, Matthew, Mark, and Luke time the Last Supper so that it was an actual Passover meal. For John, however, Jesus is the new Passover Lamb who brings a new exodus from sin and death.

As if to close the Passion narrative on one last note of irony, John has Nicodemus appear on the scene and join Joseph of Arimathea to claim Jesus' body and give it a proper burial. Regarding Joseph, we are told only that he was a "secret" believer (19:38), leaving us to wonder still whether Nicodemus was also a believer. The meaning of John's designation of Jesus' grave as a "new tomb" (19:41) is probably simple: If Jesus' body was the only one in the tomb, there would be no argument that the risen Christ was another body restored.

THE GARDEN OF GOOD

Just as Nicodemus came out of the darkness to meet with Jesus at the beginning of the Gospel, here at the close Mary Magdalene comes to the tomb while both the earth and her soul are in darkness. After she finds the tomb empty, she immediately goes and informs Peter and "the other disciple" (20:2). They have a foot race to the tomb, where Peter enters and only confirms Mary's assertion that the tomb is empty. However, the other disciple "saw and believed" (20:9). What the other disciple believed we are not told, but we may assume that this unnamed disciple had confidence that Jesus' absence has to do with God's action.

The two disciples go home; but Mary cannot tear herself away. Still weeping, she enters the tomb again and confronts two angels who ask her why she is weeping. Outside again another voice asks the same question. Perhaps she just didn't expect it; perhaps she thought it impossible; perhaps she was pre-occupied with the worry that Jesus' body had been stolen. For whatever reason, she does not recognize the risen Christ. Notice that Mary says more or less the same thing to the two male disciples (20:2), to the two angels (20:13), and to Christ (20:15): "They have taken away my Lord, and I do not know where they have laid him." Mary is one of the sheep whose shepherd knows her by name (10:3). So, when she asks Jesus her question, he speaks her name, and she recognizes who it is. John's point is crucial: Disciples of Jesus know and are known by the risen Christ.

Mary apparently reaches out to hold Jesus, but he orders her not to hold on (or to keep holding on) to him because he has not yet ascended (20:16-17). Mary learns what we all must learn: We cannot hold on to Jesus and keep him to ourselves. The risen Christ has another mission. He asks Mary to go to his followers and tell them he is risen and is ascending to God. Mary becomes the first apostle (that is, one sent out); indeed, she is the apostle to the apostles (she is sent to those who will be sent out).

LOCK THE DOORS

Mary was weeping in sorrow when the risen Christ appeared to her. The disciples now are petrified that they will be arrested for their relationship with Jesus—so fearful that they have locked the doors. Still, the risen Christ suddenly appears to them in their need. He shows them his wounds from the crucifixion to assuage any suspicion that he is a ghost or an illusion. This was important to the early church since their claims that Jesus was raised from the dead were surely attacked. Just as important, though, in this passage is what the risen Christ offers the disciples. First, almost as a reminder, Jesus promises them his peace (20:19). Then he confers upon them his own mission: They are to be sent out as God sent Jesus (20:21). Next, he empowers them through the gift of the Holy Spirit (20:22). And lastly, he bestows upon them the responsibility to offer forgiveness (20:23). These four gifts are the core of the mission of Jesus' disciples in any age. They highlight the importance of a right relationship with God, the connection between the disciples' ministry and Jesus' ministry (see also 17:18), the assurance of the Spirit's presence, and the significance of offering to people the forgiveness of Christ. John seems clearly determined to emphasize to his readers how vital it is that they acknowledge themselves as being sent for the same purpose as Jesus (John 3:16-17).

DON'T YOU BELIEVE IT!

Thomas gets a lot of bad press because of a few brief verses in John (20:24-29). He has even been nicknamed for his doubt. But imagine yourself coming back to your friends and hearing the kind of story Thomas was told. "Ah, come on now!" Thomas quite rightly wants some kind of tangible evidence—even physical touching—of his own rather than just hearsay. His friends say they have *seen* the Lord. It is only natural that Thomas should say, "Unless *I see*..." (20:25, italics added for emphasis). Mary was sorrowful. The disciples were fearful. Now Thomas is doubtful.

Finally, after eight days (or after the second Sunday, the first day of the week), Jesus appears to his followers for a third time, and Thomas has his chance. Again Jesus greets his disciples with "peace" but then turns to Thomas and invites him to touch his wounds and believe. John does not say whether or not Thomas does actually touch Jesus before he cries out, "My Lord and my God!" (20:28). Yet his confession of faith is important in several ways. First, at the near end of the Gospel, he calls Jesus "God," just as the prologue to the Gospel does (1:1). Declarations that Jesus is God provide bookends to the whole narrative. Second, Thomas uses a title ("My Lord and my God!") often employed in the Greek translation of the Old Testament (for example, Psalm 35:24) and claimed by the Roman Caesar Domitian (*ca.* 81–96 A.D.). Thomas's words became the central affirmation of the early church.

However, Jesus' response to Thomas's confession is perhaps even more important. He asks Thomas, "Have you believed because you have seen me?" Then, he announces the beatitude that may be the high point of John's Gospel: "Blessed are those who have not seen and yet have come to believe" (20:29). Jesus' words claim that those of us who live after Jesus' time are *more blessed* by God than those who experienced Christ's physical incarnation. With these words, John's Gospel has strengthened the church in every age.

WHY WRITE THIS GOSPEL?

Scholars have long wondered what the Gospel of John purports to do. Is it intended for non-Christians in the hope that, having read this book, they would believe in Christ? Or is it written for those who are already Christians to strengthen their faith and empower them for ministry? The answer seems to be given in 20:31, which says these signs are written "that you may come to believe." However, there is a tiny problem of enormous significance. Of the ancient Greek documents on which John is based, one of the oldest and most respected at this point does say "that you may *come* to believe." However, the Greek of another equally valued manuscript reads "that you may *continue* to believe." The difference is the presence or absence of one letter—the Greek sigma, or "s." Here's something to consider: In traditional practice, the Gospel is distributed to non-Christian readers so that they may be brought to faith. But it is also studied intensely by many of us who hope to strengthen our faith. In truth, the Gospel functions both ways and thus calls into question whether or not its original purpose matters.

INVITATION TO DISCIPLESHIP

We cannot help but wish that we could "come and see" as the first disciples did. However, we are left with the task of learning to believe without seeing. Suppose you are trying to convince a friend to come with you and see the beautiful sunset over the Grand Canyon. If you have actually seen it, there is little doubt that you believe it is beautiful. However, even if you can only take the witness of your friend as truth, you can also believe it is a beautiful sight.

Our discipleship is indebted to those whose faith has coaxed us into believing. We stand on the shoulders of the many saints who have brought us to this point of wanting to commit our energies to Christ's mission in the world. Therefore, discipleship is grounded on the discipleship of others, and still others will ground their mission on ours. So goes the life of the community and the communion of saints.

FOR REFLECTION

- When we compare the accounts of Jesus' trial in the four Gospels, we find that John spends an unusual amount of time on Pilate's determination of Jesus' guilt or innocence. How do you account for this? What is John's special interest in Pilate?

- According to John's story of Jesus' passion, Jesus seems in control of all the tragic events just as he was in control of his ministry. (For instance, he is strong enough to carry his cross.) How does this portrayal of Jesus affect your understanding of his humanity and his divinity? To what extent does this call into question the nature or purpose of his suffering?

- What relevance do the Resurrection appearances have for us today in our discipleship? We (usually) do not see the risen Lord but only hear about him. Where would you look for evidence of the risen Christ among us?

FOR FURTHER REFLECTION

In the movie version of the musical drama *Godspell*, after the Crucifixion scene, the Resurrection is represented in an unusual way. The disciples come walking down the street singing and carrying the body of Jesus on their shoulders. They turn a corner, and as the camera follows, the scene shifts to a crowd in the bustling main street of a big city. Horns are honking; buses speed by; shoppers and business people mill about. The disciples and their Master are no longer visible; only their singing remains. At this point, the movie ends. What value does this contemporary expression of the Resurrection have? Do you see anything in this sort of "Resurrection scene" that rings true for you? How would you interpret it?

Do You See Him?

Just after daybreak, Jesus stood on the beach; but the disciples did not know that it was Jesus.... That disciple whom Jesus loved said to Peter, "It is the Lord!"

—*John 21:4, 7*

INTRODUCTION

Isn't it interesting that after the risen Christ has appeared to the disciples a number of times, they return to their vocations as fishermen? Why would they do that? Imagine meeting the living Christ in such a personal and intimate way as the first disciples did. How would that experience have affected us? What is it about an encounter with the living Christ that would drive us back to our regular vocations? Because it is precisely there that Jesus calls us to live out our discipleship. Once the bread has been broken and the prayers have been offered, disciples of the risen Christ are needed in the everyday places of the world, particularly in the work places—be they a fishing boat, an office, a construction site, a school, or a home.

DAILY ASSIGNMENTS

DAY ONE: John 21:1-19

Why does Peter dive into the water and swim to shore as soon as he realizes the stranger is Jesus? How does this act compare to other acts of Peter? Of what importance is the number of fish caught? What is the point of the dialogue between Jesus and Peter in 21:15-19?

DAY TWO: John 21:20-25

Why does Peter ask Jesus about "the disciple whom Jesus loved"? How do you understand 21:23? What does the following verse mean in saying, "This is the disciple who is testifying to these things..."? To whom might "this disciple" refer? What is the purpose of 21:24-26, given the fact that there is an earlier conclusion at the end of Chapter 20?

DAY THREE:

Read the commentary in the participant book.

DAY FOUR:

Reread John 1–12. This time read not for the details but rather to get a sense of the overall sweep of John's story and to see the picture of Jesus that John is trying to reveal.

DAY FIVE:

Reread John 13–20. Again, read not for the details but rather to get a sense of the overall sweep of John's story and to see the picture of Jesus that John is trying to reveal.

DAY SIX:

Review the "Invitation to Discipleship" sections for all eleven sessions.

GONE FISHIN'

John 21 has been the subject of many discussions and the center of an ongoing debate. The main question is whether this chapter is a part of the original Gospel and, if not, why it was added. It seems anti-climactic to add another story after the decisive ending of the book in 20:30-31. Some commentators think Chapter 21 is an appendix written by whoever wrote Chapters 1–20. Others think it was a later addition to the Gospel by a different writer. So, should readers see it as part of the whole narrative or treat it entirely separately? In a way, it doesn't matter. The chapter stands before us as part of John's Gospel now and, regardless of how it came to be, deserves out attention.

The setting for the narrative in this chapter is the Sea of Tiberias (or Galilee—see John 6:1) and is the only Resurrection appearance to have occurred in Galilee. Peter announces he is going fishing; however, his all-night fishing trip ends unsuccessful. Imagine the disappointment of professional fishermen! Not even a bite. Then a stranger on the shore dares to give the experts some directions.

Note that Jesus corners the disciples so that they must admit their failure (21:5). Only after they have filled their nets with fish does the beloved disciple recognize Jesus, and the impulsive Peter leaps into the water and swims to shore, leaving the others to row the heavy, fish-laden boat back to land. There awaiting them is a meal of fish and bread. They drag their fishnet on land, and to their surprise it contains a hundred and fifty-three fish! Why the specific number? Is it just to emphasize how big the catch was, or is there some symbolic meaning to the number? Is it the number of kinds of fish known at the time? Is 153 the "perfect number" since it is the sum of adding all the numbers between 1 and 17? Or is it a mystery? Could it be that it means simply a whole lot of fish?

More questions abound. Why do none of the disciples dare ask Jesus who he is? Had Jesus' appearance changed that dramatically, or is it more likely the disciples hardly dared to think it was their Lord? Recall in Luke 24:15-16 that the disciples at first do not recognize the risen Lord, even though they walk alongside him to Emmaus. Is this story, as some have suggested, a kind of Eucharistic service by the shore? Why does John 21:14 say this is the *third* time Jesus appears when he has already made three appearances: first, to Mary at the tomb (20:11-18); second, to the disciples with Thomas absent (20:19-23); and then, to the disciples with Thomas present (20:26-29)?

Whatever the answers may be, there is no question that in this chapter, Jesus has once again appeared to the disciples when they are in need. When Jesus appeared previously, it was in the midst of Mary's sorrow, then as the disciples huddled in fear, and again to assuage Thomas's doubt. This time he appears on the occasion of their embarrassing failure as fishermen. John seems determined to drive home the point to his readers that Christ's nearness coincides with their neediness. It is a point John's readers still need to hear.

HOW DO I LOVE YOU?

The dialogue between Jesus and Peter in 21:15-19 tells an interesting story. Jesus asks Peter if he loves his Lord more than his colleagues do, which is an odd question. Who or what are the "these" to which Jesus refers? Do you love me more that these other disciples love me? Or do you love me more than you love your companions? Three times Jesus asks Peter if he loves him, and three times Peter responds affirmatively. Clearly the three questions and Peter's responses parallel Peter's three denials during Jesus' trials. By his affirmations of love for Jesus, Peter may compensate (to some degree) for his earlier cowardice. But the language is fascinating. In his first two questions, Jesus uses the Greek word *agapē* (A-GA-PAY), a word that defines love as free and without any expectation

Love

Translates three different Greek words. *Eraō* (E-RAH-OH—never used in John) refers to sensual, sexual love. It is the root of our word *erotic*. *Philia* (F-LEE-AH) refers to friendship love. *Agapē* (A-GA-PAY) is love that is free and without any expectation of its being returned. In John 3:16, God's love is of the *agapē* kind. Here in John 21, Jesus asks Peter if he loves him. In the first question (21:15), Jesus asks Peter if he loves him with *agapē*, and Peter responds by saying, "Yes, Lord; you know that I love [*philia*] you." In 21:16, the same words are used, but in 21:17, Jesus uses *philia*, and Peter responds with the same word.

of return, the sort of love the New Testament employs to describe God's love (see John 3:16). However, in the first two responses, Peter uses another word for love, *phileō* (PH-LE-OH), which refers to friendship love. In the third question, Jesus asks Peter if he loves him using the verb *phileō*. While Peter's response appears guarded, Jesus asks that he love his Lord with both kinds of love. In response to Jesus' question "Do you love me?" using both words for love, Peter's answer is always with the word *phileō*.

Jesus' three questions and Peter's response are each followed by commands in this order: "Feed my lambs," "tend my sheep," and "feed my sheep" (21:15-17). Jesus asks Peter to be the sort of shepherd called "the good shepherd" in John 10. Jesus then describes the sacrifice Peter will be asked to make as a commissioned shepherd. John 21:18 refers to Peter's death, which historical sources confirm. All this concludes with a simple invitation to discipleship: "Follow me"—this time to the cross.

WHERE LOVE LEADS US

It's Peter's turn to ask the questions, and he wants to know the destiny of the beloved disciple. Jesus' response really isn't an answer at all: "If it is my will that he remain until I come, what is that to you? Follow me!" There seems to have been an idea circulating that the beloved disciple would live until Christ returned, but that does not prove to be the case. We seem to be dealing here with some historical tradition in John's church, but not one we can understand. The word translated as "remain" is one we have encountered before and means to "abide" or to "dwell." In truth, we don't know what this remark means. What we *do* know is the command. None too politely, Jesus says Peter should mind his own business and pursue his own commission. Good advice for us as well.

ANOTHER ENDING?

The conclusion of the Gospel in John 20:30-31 seems sufficient, so what is the purpose of this second ending in 21:24-25? These words seem to identify the author with the beloved disciple. Is this mysterious, unnamed disciple our author? Not necessarily, because the Greek expression translated as "written" can mean a number of things besides the act of recording on paper. The same expression has been used to say "was the cause of the writing" without identifying the actual writer. The verb was used to suggest cause rather than strict activity. The best example is in 1 Corinthians 4:14 and 14:37, where the verb *to write* is used, even though Paul is clearly dictating the words. Contrast these passages with Galatians 6:11, where Paul says, "See what large letters I make when I am writing in my own hand!" At the very least, it seems these words are here to encourage us to believe that the beloved disciple was the inspiration or the ultimate source of the Gospel, or at least Chapter 21.

INVITATION TO DISCIPLESHIP

John 21 invites us to become disciples or strengthen our discipleship. It concludes the Gospel with another story of a Resurrection appearance, this time coming in the context of the common human experience of what we might call a professional failure, one that results in sorrow, fear, and doubt. Christian discipleship, then, entails a conviction that Christ remains active in our world today through the agency of those who believe in him. When we see the hungry fed, the ill healed, the lonely befriended, and the depressed uplifted, we see the risen Christ at work.

Following Jesus means more than simply acknowledging that Christ fulfills the basic needs of humans. It means becoming actively engaged in seeking to fulfill those needs today—that is, we become the hands, the words, and the deed of Christ today. That is part of our "coming and seeing." However, we should not conclude that we must somehow transcend our human tendencies to fail. Recognizing our propensity to fail in our mission for Christ is one of the reasons we are part of a community, the church. We share fish around the fire with other disciples but then move out into the wider world to serve. According to John's Gospel, when we move out from within the community of disciples, we are guided by several principles.

First, as John makes clear, every believer is a disciple. As we have already said, because the word *disciple* is often used today to identify the twelve who were Jesus' followers, we may think this is true in John. However, that identification is denied, as John 6:60-71 indicates. Those verses tell us that some of Jesus' disciples deserted him (6:66). Then, Jesus turns to the "twelve" and addresses them (6:67). Those twelve are a distinct group within the larger category of disciples. As a consequence of this broadening of the word *disciple*, we can no longer say who exactly was present for Jesus' foot washing, heard the Farewell Discourses, or witnessed the appearance of the risen Christ in John 20. What difference does this make for us? It means all Christians are disciples, and we cannot exempt ourselves on the basis that a commandment or mission was meant strictly for the twelve and not us.

Second, discipleship is rooted in the identity of Christ. There isn't another biblical document that devotes as much of its content to who Jesus was and is as does John. The Gospel of John was the most influential book of the Bible in guiding the ancient church to define many basic Christian beliefs. According to John, disciples are sent into the world just as God sent Jesus into the world (17:18; 20:21). We are to love one another as Christ loves us (15:12). We are to be one, just as Jesus and God are one (17:11); and we are not of the world, just as Jesus is not of the world (17:16). Who we are as disciples arises from who Christ is.

Third, disciples are united as a single body with one another because God and Christ are one (17:20-21). Hence, the unity of the church is not a matter of organizational structure but a matter of our understanding of who Christ was and is. We are one with one another at levels far deeper than acquaintance or friendship. Our devotion to Christ and God is singular, and our mission to the world is singular. So our unity is not, as some would say today, full agreement on ethical and moral issues. It is Christ who makes us one.

Fourth, as Christ manifests God's glory in the world, so disciples manifest the same glory (17:22-23). Remember that *glory* (the Greek word *doxa*, DOCS-AH) is the presence of God in the world. Therefore, our discipleship shows God to the world. In John, of course, God's glory is clearly love.

Fifth, disciples are part of a divine community in which all the parties are related to the others. The metaphor of the vine and branches makes clear that Christ remains in us as we remain in him (15:4). This simple diagram may help us grasp the meaning of such a view of the church.

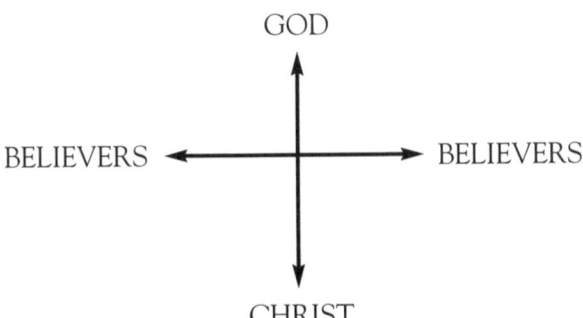

Sixth, our mission as disciples is to follow Christ and to serve others in love. This is obvious, of course, but we need to be reminded of it again and again. Today it is easy to become preoccupied with church growth or institutional welfare and forget that we are not so much commissioned to grow in numbers as we are to grow in serving. Discipleship means putting the welfare of others above our own. For instance, we cannot ignore world hunger when we live in a nation where obesity is a major problem.

Seventh, disciples are required to continue their growth in understanding and commitment. One of the features of John's portrayal of the disciples is that at one point they seem to start to understand Jesus. But then Jesus prods them to seek further understanding. The Paraclete is the source of that further insight. As Jesus promised the disciples, the Paraclete "will teach you everything, and remind you of all that I have said to you" (14:26). As disciples, we are always believers on our way to greater understanding of the Christ we follow.

Finally, disciples may expect the same response as that which Jesus received. This is made clear in John 15:18-25; 16:2b, 32-33; and 17:14. Likewise, Peter's destiny, as described in 21:18-19, sounds much like Jesus' destiny: "You will stretch out your hands, and someone else will fasten a belt around you and take you where you do not wish to go." We must be cautious because we cannot equate just any rejection by others as the result of our discipleship. Nor can we seek suffering for its own sake, thinking that if we suffer, we must be faithful. This means we may need to take unpopular stands. We may feel compelled by our Christian beliefs to hold minority views. We no more look for suffering than Jesus did, but it may come nonetheless.

FOR REFLECTION

- Besides the eight just mentioned in the "Invitation to Discipleship" section, what features of discipleship do you find especially important or emphasized in the Gospel of John?

- The disciples in the boat are not sure who the stranger on the shore is. Only after they catch a net full of fish do they recognize Jesus. When have you encountered the risen Christ in another person but did not realize it at the time? How do you discern the presence of Christ in another person?

- Jesus asks Peter three times if Peter loves him (21:15-17). Each time, after Peter has declared his love for him, Jesus responds with a similar command: "Feed my lambs," "tend my sheep," and "feed my sheep." The specific language of these commands varies, but the meaning is the same. How is the service Jesus asks of Peter related to Peter's love for him? What other ways can we express our love for Christ besides in service to other people?

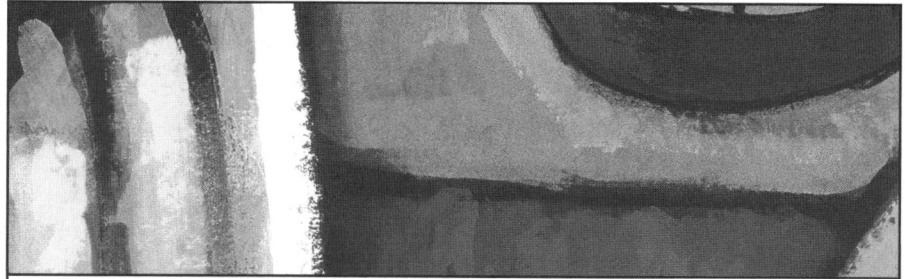

FOR FURTHER REFLECTION

The late Henri Nouwen, a Roman Catholic priest, teacher, and writer, wrote the following when he was preparing to leave Lima, Peru, and return to the United States:

> I look forward to going home tomorrow, to sitting in a comfortable airplane. I like being welcomed home by friends. I look forward to being back again in my cozy apartment, with my books, my paintings, and my plants.... But is it there that I will find God?
>
> Or is God in this dusty, dry, cloud-covered city of Lima, in this confusing, unplanned, and often chaotic conglomeration of people, dogs, and houses? Is God perhaps where the hungry kids play, the old ladies beg, and the shoeshine boys pick your pocket?
>
> I surely have to be where God is. I have to become obedient to God, listen to God's voice, and go wherever that voice calls me. Even when I do not like it, even when it is not a way of cleanliness or comfort. (From *Seeds of Hope: A Henri Nouwen Reader*, edited by Robert Durback [Doubleday, 1997]; pages 140–41.)

How do these words relate to your discipleship?

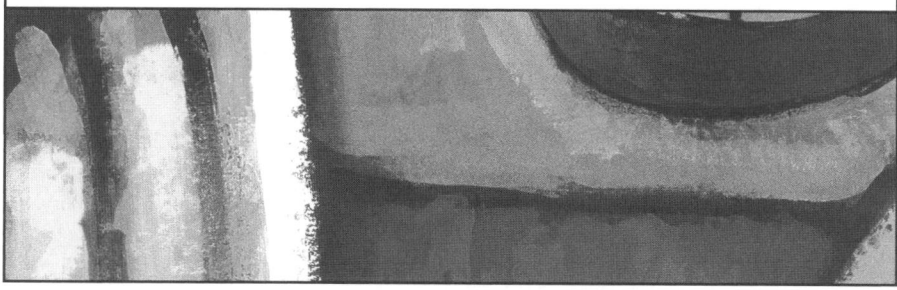